METHODICAL DRESSAGE

OF THE

RIDING HORSE

From The last teaching of François Baucher

As recalled by one of his students:

General François Faverot de Kerbrech

And

DRESSAGE

OF THE

OUTDOOR HORSE

Recalled by one of his students:

General George de Lagarenne

Copyright 2010 by Xenophon Press LLC

All rights reserved. No part of this work may be reproduced or transmitted in any form or by any means, electronic or mechanical, including photocopying, or by any information storage or retrieval system except by a written permission from the publisher.

Published by Xenophon Press LLC, 7518 Bayside Road, Franktown, Virginia 23354-2106, U.S.A.

XenophonPress@gmail.com

www.XenophonPress.com

Print book

ISBN-10   0933316178

ISBN-13   9780933316171

Edited by Richard and Frances Williams

Translated by Michael L. M. Fletcher

e-book

ISBN-10   0933316186

ISBN-13   9780933316188

METHODICAL DRESSAGE
of the
RIDING HORSE

From The last teaching of François Baucher

As recalled by one of his students:

By General François Faverot de Kerbrech

And

DRESSAGE
of the
OUTDOOR HORSE

Recalled by one of his students:

By General George de Lagarenne

Xenophon Press Library

Xenophon Press is dedicated to the preservation of classical equestrian literature. We bring both new and old works to English-speaking riders. Available at www.XenophonPress.com

30 Years with Master Nuno Oliveira, Henriquet 2011
A New Method to Dress Horses, Cavendish 2015
A Rider's Survival from Tyranny, de Kunffy 2012
Another Horsemanship, Racinet 1994
Art of the Lusitano, Yglesias de Oliveira 2012
Austrian Art of Riding, Poscharnigg 2015
Breaking and Riding, Fillis 2015
Baucher and His School, Decarpentry 2011
Dressage in the French Tradition, Diogo de Bragança 2011
Dressage Principles Illuminated Expanded Ed. de Kunffy 2015
École de Cavalerie Part II, Robichon de la Guérinière 1992, 2015
Equine Osteopathy: What the Horses Have Told Me, Ginaux 2014
François Baucher: The Man and His Method, Baucher/Nelson 2013
Great Horsewomen of the 19th Century in the Circus, Nelson 2015
Gymnastic Exercises for Horses Volume II, Russell 2013
H. Dv. 12 Cavalry Manual of Horsemanship, Reinhold 2014
Handbook of Jumping Essentials, Lemaire de Ruffieu 1997
Handbook of Riding Essentials, Lemaire de Ruffieu 2015
Healing Hands, Giniaux, DVM 1998
Horse Training: Outdoors and High School, Beudant 2014
Legacy of Master Nuno Oliveira, Millham 2013
Manege Moderne, D'Eisenberg 2015
Methodical Dressage of the Riding Horse, Faverot de Kerbrech 2010
Racinet Explains Baucher, Racinet 1997
Science and Art of Riding in Lightness, Stodulka 2015
The Art and Science of Riding in Lightness, Stodulka 2014
The Art of Traditional Dressage, Volume I DVD, de Kunffy 2013
The Ethics and Passions of Dressage Expanded Ed., de Kunffy 2013
The Gymnasium of the Horse, Steinbrecht 2011
The Italian Tradition of Equestrian Art, Tomassini 2014
The Maneige Royal, de Pluvinel 2010
The Portuguese School of Equestrian Art, de Oliveira/da Costa 2012
The Spanish Riding School & Piaffe and Passage, Decarpentry 2013
To Amaze the People with Pleasure and Delight, Walker 2015
Total Horsemanship, Racinet 1999
Wisdom of Master Nuno Oliveira, de Coux 2012

Table of Contents

Translator's Acknowledgements — vii
Foreword to the Translation — ix
Foreword by the Author — xi

Methodical Dressage of the Riding Horse — 1
DEFINITIONS — 1
THE GOAL OF DRESSAGE — 2
General Principles — 3
    I. LIGHTNESS AND THE *RAMENER* — 3
    II. OBEDIENCE TO THE LEG AND THE
    "*EFFET D'ENSEMBLE*" ON THE SPUR — 10
    III. THE STRAIGHT HORSE — 13
    IV. DESCENT OF THE HAND AND LEG — 15
    V. THE *RASSEMBLER* — 16

PROGRESSION OF DRESSAGE — 19

PART ONE: PREPARATION — 19

CHAPTER I: FLEXIONS, WORK WITH THE WHIP, USE
    OF THE LUNGE WHIP — 19
CHAPTER II: THE EQUITATION OF FANTASY
    -ARTIFICIAL GAITS (AIRS) — 35
CHAPTER III: THE FIRST LESSON IN MOUNTING — 40
CHAPTER IV: REPEATING THE WORK TAUGHT
    IN HAND WITH AN AIDE IN THE SADDLE,
    LESSON OF THE SPUR — 44

PART TWO: PREPARATION Continued — 50

GENERAL RECOMMENDATIONS — 50
CHAPTER I PREPARATORY WORK
    IN THE MIDDLE OF THE SCHOOL — 54
CHAPTER II: AT THE WALK — 57
CHAPTER III: AT THE COLLECTED TROT — 68
CHAPTER IV: THE *RASSEMBLER* — 73

PART THREE: PUTTING IT TOGETHER   75

CHAPTER I: DEPARTS AND WORK AT THE CANTER   75
CHAPTER II: THE LENGTHENED TROT
(*Grand trot*, Large trot)   89
CHAPTER III: CHANGES OF LEAD AT THE CANTER   91
CHAPTER IV: THE *GALOP ALLONGÉ* (Extended Canter) 98
CHAPTER V: JUMPING OBSTACLES   99
CHAPTER VI: HABITUATING THE HORSE TO NOISES
OF WAR AND TO OTHER FEARSOME OBJECTS   100
CHAPTER VII: FANCY EQUITATION-ARTIFICIAL AIRS 101
CHAPTER VIII: FANCY EQUITATION-Continued   105

PART FOUR: CONFIRMING THE HORSE   108

CHAPTER I: *RAMENER OUTRÉ*   108
CHAPTER II: THE LITTLE *ATTAQUES*   111
CONCLUSION   114

Dressage of the Outdoor Horse   117

Foreword   *119*
INTRODUCTION   123
PROGRESSION   125
   1. WORK IN HAND   125
   2. LESSON IN MOUNTING   126
   3. WORKING THE HORSE IN PLACE 127
   4. WORK AT THE WALK   130
   5. WORK AT THE COLLECTED TROT 136
   6. WORK AT THE CANTER   137
   7. WORK AT THE LENGTHENED TROT 139
   8. CHANGE OF LEAD AT THE CANTER 139
   9. EXERCISE AT THE *GALLOP RAPIDE* 140
   10. THE *ROULER*   141
CONCLUSION   143
GLOSSARY   145
BIBLIOGRAPHY   147

Translator's Acknowledgements

The translator wishes to thank some very special people without whom this project would not have been completed.

Nicole Langford gave me unconditional love, support, and encouragement when I needed to recover from devastating illness and loss, and gave me the opportunity to recover the language of my mother.

Cecilia Thompson assumed that I would complete the project once started, wanted to see results in a predicted time, and helped me with some challenging idiomatic expressions.

Jean-Louis Lombart, student of Colonel André Jousseaume was my teacher for eight years. He gave me the opportunity to learn the equitation of France informed by Baucher, L'Hotte, Raabe, Faverot de Kerbrech, and Beudant on horses that he trained. He provided indispensable help with the translation of equestrian idiom. He gave me his invaluable friendship, and often lent me rare French books on equitation.

Major Miguel Tavora, student of Nuno Oliveira, gave me a firm grounding in the application of the principles of Steinbrecht and the gymnasticising of a horse, leavened by Baucherist lightness, my introduction to the Second "Manner." He also provided me an outstanding example of a master horse trainer.

Gil Merrick encouraged my curiosity for French equitation even as we practiced the principles of Steinbrecht.

Patrick Burssens introduced me to riding in lightness, and lit an ember that never died out. Jean-Claude Racinet gave me his personal encouragement in my quest to understand equitation and horsemanship.

Susan Racinet was very kind and generous with her time. Amy Fletcher gave her father her quiet love and support. Cheryl Chernicky gave me her generous support. Jeff Channing and Staci Jones gave me their support and generously provided opportunities for me to ride.

Ivan Bezugloff, founder of *Dressage and CT* and Xenophon Press, encouraged me to complete this work on the Second "Manner." Richard and Frances Williams, current Publishers of Xenophon Press, generously agreed to publish the work and provided extensive editorial assistance.

I am very grateful to them all.

-Michael L. M. Fletcher

Foreword to the Translation

The teaching of François Baucher was in constant evolution. Every new discovery would eclipse the old one, but if some techniques could change, the principles and objectives were maintained. He published several editions of his book, *Method of Equitation*. His Method became known as First Manner and Second Manner. The Second Manner appeared for the first time in the twelfth edition in the last part of the book that he called *New Equestrian Ways*.

The Second Manner of the Method was fully exposed by General Faverot de Kerbrech, a loyal student of Baucher in his book *Dressage Methodique du Cheval de Selle, D'Apres les Deniers Enseignements de Baucher*. There exist translations in English of the books exposing Baucher's First Manner but none of the book by Faverot de Kerbrech.

Michael Fletcher has applied himself with great determination in translating the aforementioned book in great detail and precision which is always difficult because there are terms and words difficult to translate. Michael Fletcher has done it in such a way that all of these words and terms become very clear for the reader to understand.

I have known Michael Fletcher for many years, first as my student and later as a constant auditor of my clinics in the USA. We owe him thanks for the possibility of now being able to study in English, for the first time, the Second Manner of Baucher's Method.

I wish to express my gratitude to Michael and hope that this remarkable book, now written in English, receives the accolades it deserves.

- Major Miguel Tavora

Foreword

The last ideas of Baucher on equitation and dressage are little known. After the dreadful accident that broke his legs, the illustrious *écuyer* could never again ride in public. He retired, and, after 1861, only taught a very few lessons. Of the rare students who followed those lessons, only two or three are still alive today (at the time of Faverot's writing).

Baucher was too old to revise into one method his various works, which had been continuously modified by new discoveries, and he was no longer able to make public a complete and methodical explanation of his last training procedures. He preferred to pose general principles contained in a few words, saying that it was up to teachers, trained directly at his school, to show how to apply these principles in the thousand particular cases that produce a living practice.

The detailed lessons of this learned master, misunderstood, unknown, or most of the time made a travesty of, are therefore threatened with disappearance without leaving a trace.

It is this threat, that made the author of this book, decide to yield to numerous requests and to publish a work which at first was not destined to see the light of day. A student of the great Baucher, the author attended many of his lessons. Admitted later into Baucher's intimacy, he saw Baucher work, and has himself ridden the last horses trained by that incomparable écuyer. Finally, the author often heard him explain the procedures of dressage, which in the master's eyes represented equestrian truth to which his fertile mind was so fixed toward the end of his life.

A fervent disciple, the author put into writing, day by day, not only the detail of the lessons that he attended, but also the diverse education arising from his friendly informal conversations with his eminent teacher.

These are the notebooks that have served as the basis for this book. The reader would do well to fix in his mind the difficulty in explaining, with only words, certain effects in dressage that are more in the domain of practice than that of theory. Furthermore, like all founders of their own school, Baucher adopted expressions that were often debatable from the point of view of science or grammar, but it is indispensable to conserve them when one is explaining his theories. They have, for him, a very distinct and very specific meaning and they would be otherwise nearly impossible to replace by others more pleasing or more exact.

Finally, it is easy to epilogue on a treatise on equitation or dressage, always unrewarding to write, but one will recall that often the smallest demonstration on the horse renders clear in an instant that which appears obscure in writing, despite long and minute explanations.

Faverot de Kerbrech

METHODICAL DRESSAGE
OF THE RIDING HORSE

DEFINITIONS

The intention of the rider is transmitted to the horse by the language of the aids. The aids communicate to the horse the requested action and position.

Action. - The *action* is the force of impulsion necessary to obtain the sought-after movement. The action brings about the thrust of the *ressorts* (springs, resources, the muscles that control the joints, including the joints of the back) that support the mass of the body.

Position. - The *position* is the normal distribution of the weight on the horse's four legs in preparation for the movement requested. Consequently and in a complementary way, the joints and limbs are used appropriately for the distribution of weight.

Movement. - Position combined with action produces *movement*, the natural result of the two generating causes. Passing from movement to inaction is also obtained by engaging the particular position that leads to or permits the annulment of the action.

Equilibrium (balance). - The ease, more or less, with which the rider modifies the distribution of weight over the four legs to produce different positions, indicates the degree of *equilibrium* or balance of the horse. The more facile the displacement of the weight in all directions, the more perfect is the balance. By virtue of this principle, one says that the horse is "in balance" when simple indications suffice for the rider to modify, at will, the distribution of the weight on the supporting legs.

THE GOAL OF DRESSAGE

What the rider seeks to accomplish. - When the rider undertakes the training of a horse, the first condition of success is to carefully consider what he seeks to obtain; that is, the qualities that he wants his horse to acquire.

These qualities can be summed up in a few words, and he should note that these are always the same, regardless of the type of service to which a mount is destined.

Any saddle horse must be rendered easy and agreeable to ride, regular in his gaits (paces), docile, willing, and as brilliant as his conformation allows.

For the horse to be "easy and agreeable to ride, regular in his gaits," it is necessary that he be well balanced, light to the hand and leg, straight in the shoulders and haunches, with his head constantly steady and (correctly) placed and that he carry himself in balance without the help of the aids. For him to be "docile, willing," all defenses, all resistance, both instinctive and voluntary, must disappear. When they reappear, they must be immediately eliminated. Finally, for him to be "as brilliant as his conformation allows," the rider must be able to seat the horse on his haunches at will, magnify his movements, and elevate the horse's gaits.

The rider's goals in dressage are:

1) To endeavor ceaselessly to obtain lightness, a very steady *ramener*

2) To train the horse to great obedience to the rider's leg

3) To strive to keep the horse constantly straight in the shoulders and the haunches

4) To teach the horse the habit of going without the help of aids

5) Moreover, he must make the horse familiar with the *rassembler*.

Hereafter, we are going to study the means by which to achieve these goals.

GENERAL PRINCIPLES

I.   LIGHTNESS AND THE *RAMENER*

Lightness. - The search for and the conservation of lightness must be the constant preoccupation of the rider.

"Lightness to the hand" means the quality of a horse that obeys the aids without leaning on the hand. The hand must not experience the sensation of weight more or less difficult to displace, nor a force that resists its action.

Lightness is recognized by the absence of resistance to the effect of the curb or the bridoon; the simple half-tension of one or of both reins must bring about the soft mobility of the lower jaw without movement of the horse's head, without a markedly apparent opening of his mouth; and the horse's tongue must make one of the bits flip above the other producing an occasional "argentine sound." Let us add that this soft mobility of the jaw should continue for some noticeable time and should not cease abruptly.

Such are the conditions that together constitute true lightness. This set of conditions is for the rider the relevant and infallible indication of the perfect balance of his horse, as long as it is sustained without change.

The consequence of the complete relaxation of the jaw is the *ramener*, which is obtained of itself, the horse's head taking, at the lightest indication of the reins, a position close to the vertical without his neck losing its self-carriage and steadiness.

At all times, whether in hand or mounted, when anything is to be asked of the horse, the rider must begin by making the horse light, by seeking the soft mobility of the jaw.

A horse cannot contract any part of himself in order to oppose the request of his rider without also contracting his jaw.

In obtaining lightness, the rider, by the very nature of the deed, makes existing resistances disappear. This favorable result continues as long as lightness persists.

Similarly, while a movement is executed or a gait is continued, the rider must frequently verify that the horse remains light.

How to ask for lightness. - Whether the rider is working in hand or mounted, there are two cases to examine when he asks for lightness.

1st-Consider that the horse is halted, standing calm and perfectly immobile.

The rider feels the mouth by gradually taking a half-tension on the reins, or one of the reins, in order to see if the jaw is flexible and mobile.

If the rider obtains lightness, but only the lightness that we have defined above, he must *give* (reduce the tension on the reins by relaxing the fingers): the horse is now in balance, he is ready to accept the action and position for any movement that might be demanded of him.

If the hand does not meet lightness as soon as it takes up a half-tension on the reins, the hand continues this half-tension *while slightly increasing the intensity*.

This "slow force" generally suffices to make the horse yield his jaw, especially if there is only a little laziness or inattention on the part of the horse.

We can say then, that this simple and mild effect constitutes *the ordinary means of obtaining lightness*. It is this effect that the rider must be able to access throughout the duration of all training.

Sometimes, despite a long wait and the persistent solicitation of the rider, the relaxation of the jaw is not produced. This indicates that there exist resistances serious enough that it will be necessary to overcome them by more efficacious procedures.

These resistances are of two kinds:

Resistances of Weight. - When the rider, in looking for lightness, has felt in his hand a sensation of dead weight, difficult to displace, we can say that he has encountered a "resistance of weight."

Resistances of Force. - When the rider has met force coming from muscular contractions of the jaw, directed instinctively or voluntarily by the horse against the action of the bit, this active resistance evokes the idea of a fight against the rider. We call that the "resistance of force."

The rider counteracts resistances of weight by the half-halt, and resistances of force by the vibration.

The half-halt. - Here is how the one can achieve the half-halt if one is mounted on the horse:

Without ceasing contact with the horse's mouth, and without drawing itself toward the rider's body, the hand contracts energetically, making a closed fist, which turns sharply, the fingers up as much as possible. Then almost instantaneously, the hand increases its action on the bit, moving upwards and backwards without jerking. ("Backwards" is accomplished by the rotation of the hand bringing the little finger up and backwards. The wrist may bend, but does not itself approach the riders's body: instead it remains fixed in place in relation to the horse's mouth.) The power of the effect is in proportion to that of the resistance it encounters.

If one is on foot (working in hand), proceed in an analogous manner, but without turning the wrist.

The half-halt can be achieved with one rein or two at the same time, likewise with either the curb or the snaffle With the half-halt, one must never make the horse move backwards.

The vibration. - The vibration is a succession of little tremors, a trembling or quivering transmitted to one of the bits, whether acting directly upon it while working in hand, or vibrating one or both of the reins of that bit from the saddle.

Like the half-halt, the vibration can be given on either the bridoon or the curb. It lasts one to several seconds, and is strong or weak in relation to the resistance met, but it must not vary in intensity during its application. It must not make the horse move backwards at all.

If the rider has met a resistance of weight, he addresses it by one or more half-halts as necessary; if it is a resistance of force, he employs the vibration, repeated several times, with equal force, if required.

Then, as soon as the rider believes the resistances to be annulled, he feels the mouth anew by giving to the reins a half-tension, which, augmented very slightly for a certain time, should bring about lightness if the resistances have effectively disappeared. This is the "proof" of the operation.

If the use of this slow force does not produce lightness in a few seconds, it is because the operation was done badly.

In that case, the rider must repeat the half-halts or vibrations, according to the resistance, but he must endeavor to increase delicacy and tact.

If the horse, while being halted, is worried or fretting, the rider must obtain, before demanding lightness, complete immobility.

Immobility is achieved by responding to any movement on the part of the horse with half-halts, proportioned in force according to the fault committed.

As soon as each half-halt is given, the rider, peacefully and without anger, studies the reaction of the horse.

If the horse leaps about or otherwise continues to resist, appearing finally to pay no attention to the correction, the rider resumes the correction energetically, several times if it is needed.

After the horse, more quiet now, seems to fear the chastisement, the half-halts become infrequent and less strong. Still, the rider continues them until obtaining immobility, accompanied by perfect calm.

Then the rider asks for lightness, as described above.

Only if the half-halts were unsuccessful in inspiring a healthy respect in a very fiery or mettlesome horse, the rider should put him in a cavesson, which he will use in hand to give the horse *saccades* (little tugs upward) following the same prescription as for the half-halts, and having an aide momentarily replace him in the saddle.

When a mounted horse has been "put on the spur," as we will explain further on, the rider can immobilize him at will by an *"effet d'ensemble* on the spur," which we will also explain further on. The preceding applies above all to a horse that the rider is starting.

2nd –Consider the horse in action.

As stated before, the rider must demand lightness in his mount before giving the horse a new position. He must also reassure himself that the jaw remains supple and mobile during the execution of movements and continuation of gaits.

The procedure for the above is the same as when the horse is halted.

If lightness arises out of a simple half-tension on the reins, as practiced at the halt, with the movement continuing with the regularity of a metronome, the rider must hasten to give (the reins).

Understanding "decomposing the force and the movement."-If the action described above, instead of bringing soft mobility of the jaw, alters the gait or the movement, or worse yet, reveals the existence of serious resistances, the rider must *halt*, immobilize the horse, and then look for lightness at the halt, as explained earlier.

The rider remains with his horse at the halt, for several minutes if necessary, until balance is re-established, at least long enough for the previous movement to "no longer resonate" in the body of the horse.

When this result (balanced, mobile jaw) has been obtained, when calm has completely returned, that is the moment to re-introduce the action and the position, which will produce anew the preceding movement or the interrupted gait.

That is what is called "decompose the force and the movement."

If, once in action, balance is again lost, the rider decomposes (de-constructs the force and the movement, usually at the halt), and restarts the action (in balance), as often as necessary.

With young horses or those little advanced in training, the rider must, at each instance, stop to re-establish balance at the halt, reproduce lightness, and renew calm and confidence. Through these moments of complete rest, the horses are spared any kind of useless fatigue.

With horses whose gaits are irregular, this recommendation is yet more important. The essential quality of a good gait is that it be perfectly regular, that each stride be in the same time as the next in tempo and cadence.

If the smallest irregularity remains, the rider must halt, and completely relax (the jaw), before departing again.

The rider must, above all, bring great attention to the *depart* (*naissance*, birth) at whatever gait so that it is immediately very free, very prompt, and very regular.

If the depart is not perfect, stop short, and decompose (the force and the movement).

Start again (in balance) as often as necessary.

According to the principle, be content with *a few strides* perfectly executed.

When the training has become more advanced, the rider should begin to overcome resistances while in motion, especially if they are not too serious.

Without halting, the rider employs the same effects that he used at the halt, but with increased tact and finesse.

It is important that the various actions of the hand must not take anything away from the force of impulsion. They must not bring about a stop, nor a slowing-down, nor any alteration whatsoever in the movement, the direction, or the gait.

II. OBEDIENCE TO THE LEG AND THE "EFFET D'ENSEMBLE" ON THE SPUR

In the same way that the horse must be light to the hand, he must also be "light to the leg." Here is what we have to understand by that term.

How the Horse must respond to the Leg. - With the horse at the halt, if the hand does not hold in opposition, a simultaneous and equal pressure of the rider's legs must produce instantaneous forward movement: with slow calm progression, if their action has been weak; with rapid, energetic, even unrestrained speed, if the effect of the legs has been accordingly strong.

When the horse is moving, the contact of the rider's calves must similarly bring about an acceleration of the gait according to their pressure.

Whether at the halt or in movement, the approach of a single leg (behind the girth) must make the croup move to the opposite side; quietly, if its action is very light; lively, if it is more marked. But since the pressure of an isolated leg, when used at the girth, also has the result of producing or accelerating the forward movement, it is essential, at least in principle, that the opposing hand make a barrier, and receive this impulsion in order to govern it. Without the opposing hand, the leg will be obliged to employ great force, only to produce an effect almost always incomplete.

When the rider applies both legs, if their simple contact does not produce or re-establish the desired action, he touches (*toucher*) the horse immediately with both spurs at the same time, without any opposition by the hand.

He repeats these little *attaques* of the spur (Translator's Note: *ces pitites attaques*, these little attacks, have been controversial in that they invite misinterpretation.

The term means "repeated touches, of increasing intensity if necessary, but not violence"), until the desired result is achieved.

In the same way, if at the approach of a single leg, the giving-way of the croup is not immediate, a pinch of the spur on the same side, coming immediately, punishes the horse for his laziness and forces him to obey.

The rider comes, by this means, to give the horse a great sensitivity (*finesse*) to the leg, to render him light to the leg, and soon the simple contact of the pant-leg or the boot suffices to obtain or augment impulsion, or if he is acting on only one flank, to displace the croup.

It is necessary in the meanwhile to redouble tact in the use of the repeated little *attaques* of the spur, and to use them only with discretion, in order not to provoke twisting of the tail.

How to put the horse "On the spur." - But *before using the spur this way*, the horse must have been brought along in his training, from the very first lessons, to accept the spur and to respond to it as follows:

If at the halt, the rider progressively applies his legs and then the spurs with just enough force, and with the hand immediately presenting opposition, the horse must remain completely immobile and conserve his lightness unaltered.

If, with the spurs resting on the hair of the coat, the rider increases their force while giving with the hand, *the horse must carry himself forward forthrightly at the walk* and remain light.

If the horse is at the walk, the graduated application of spurs must alter neither the gait nor the lightness when the hand makes an opposition.

If the pressure of the spurs is increased, and the hand gives, the horse *must take up the trot without abruptness*.

Finally, following the same principle, *he must depart forthrightly on the spur from the trot, from the walk, or even from the halt, at the lengthened (grand) trot.*

Then the horse "knows the spur," the contact of the aid no longer scares him, and, on the contrary, causes a certain surprised attention that calms him and permits obtaining a tranquil impulsion as needed, or a more powerful impulsion if necessary.

He is ready to receive the little *attaques*, which from then on, absent the opposition of the hand, *always make him direct his forces forward*, thus destroying any tendency to back up or "get behind the aids" (*acculement*).

Finally, from this moment on when it is necessary, it becomes possible for the rider to enclose, or imprison his pupil between the bit and the spur. In this fashion, the rider extinguishes in the horse's mind any idea of defense. By bringing the bridle hand closer to the body (by rotating his wrist), and closing the legs rapidly and progressively up to a firm, continued, and energetic pressure of both spurs, the rider produces what we call the "*effet d'ensemble on the spur.*"

This effect brings about, or confirms, the relaxation of the horse's jaw, destroys any resistance, and immobilizes the horse at the will of the rider, or if the rider makes the action of the spur predominant while softening the opposition of his hand without letting the head escape, this effect obliges the horse to keep the gait at which he is moving, whenever the vaguest idea of revolt is manifested.

The rider is thus *absolutely the master of any defence,* and is able to ride his horse *wherever he wants, and at any gait he wishes,* no matter what the horse's contrary impulse, nor whatever might frighten him.

The horse perceives quickly that it is impossible to resist the rider. A feeling of powerlessness brings him to give up the fight. His state of mind is tamed, and he resigns himself to obey.

It is thus that we can surely and radically cure the most dangerous and inveterate rebelliousness (*rétivité*).

III.　THE STRAIGHT HORSE

How to shift the weight of the neck towards the opposite shoulder. - When the horse is light and in the *ramener* (or "on the bit"), a half-tension on the right rein in the direction of the left haunch should bring, without changing the lightness, the end of the his nose to the right, and lift, arch, and shift his neck to the left because of the inclination of his head.

The right shoulder is thus lightened, preparing it to be lifted; on the other hand, with the weight of the neck being shifted to left, the forehand has a tendency to "fall" to the left; that is, to move in that direction and the croup is flexed towards the right. The horse is then slightly bent in a circle, the end of his nose and his haunches to the right.

The half-tension on the left rein should produce the inverse effect in *perfect symmetry*.

It is necessary to strive for this result and to repeat these effects on the reins often, at the halt and at all gaits, to accomplish these "inclinations" with equal facility to both the right and the left, as they frequently find their application in dressage.

One of the greatest of equestrian difficulties is the achievement and conservation, without fail, of strict straightness of the horse in his shoulders and haunches.

This condition is essential for the horse to be in balance. But, nearly all horses are more or less bent to one side, whether by a natural predisposition, or by bad habits acquired when they began to be ridden.

The consequence of this bend is to throw more weight on to one shoulder, and to make the opposite haunch arch forward.

The horse thus finds himself physically well disposed for defense against, or at least for resistance to, certain effects of the rider. It is, therefore, important to correct this unruly attitude as soon as possible.

How to straighten a horse. - The simplest and most practical way to accomplish straightness is to teach the horse to take up the opposite bend at the will of the rider.

It is then, in being able to make these two "inclinations" with equal facility to the right and to the left, that one may come to straighten a horse that has a tendency to bend himself to one side; but these inclinations must be obtained by the hand alone, with the horse remaining light and having his head placed (in ramener).

It is important to try not to use the legs. For example, in the diagonal effect which acts on the hindquarters and displaces them, the horse's hindquarters often revert to their original position when the action of the opposing leg ceases, which constitutes work without result.

To sum up, the rider must not, in the above case, mobilize the croup around the forehand. It is the transfer of weight from one shoulder to the other, produced by the indirect rein, *la rêne d'appui*, that is closer in similarity,

but more subtle so as not to make the horse turn, to the modern 4th rein effect, the counter-rein of opposition in front of the withers, than to the modern 2nd rein effect, also called *"rêne d'appui."* (Licart, *Assiette et Emploi des Aides*, Fédération Française de Sports Équestres, undated, pages 13-16)), that bends the horse slightly in the direction opposite his original inclination.

It appears, in fact, that the haunches, like the end of the horse's nose, are shifted to the opposite side while only the shoulders, in yielding to the hand, are slightly inclined in the direction in which the weight of the neck has been brought to "fall."

This method, given to counter the particular tendency of a horse to take on an imbedded bend, in no way relieves the rider from paying constant attention to placing and keeping his pupil very straight in the shoulders and the haunches at all gaits, at the halt, and in the rein-back, despite the demands of training.

IV. "DESCENT OF THE HAND AND LEG"

The horse, whether at the halt or in movement, should preserve, by himself, the position given to him by the rider as long as the rider does not modify it.

Equally, when he is in movement, the horse's impulsion should continue without alteration until the rider, at his wish, augments, diminishes, or annuls its intensity.

Bringing the horse along as quickly as possible to go without the help of the aids (self carriage). - In addition, one of the rider's preoccupations throughout the training must be to teach the horse to do without the help of the aids, hand, leg, whip, click of the tongue, etc. The horse should be left as free as possible (in self carriage), as long as he holds his balance; that is, as long as the lightness does not change, the head remains steady, the neck supports itself, and the gait continues without change.

So, as soon as he can, and from then on, at any moment, the rider must try the "descent of the hand and leg." (Descent of the hand: release the finger pressure, augmented as needed by rotating the wrist with the little finger toward the horse, and lower the hand, breaking the contact; descent of the leg: release the leg pressure, letting the leg remain in resting contact.)

The descent of the hand is cut short and left incomplete as soon as the neck lowers, the head loses its steadiness or balance is upset in any way whatever. The rider must then take up the reins or apply the leg to oppose any displacement of the head or neck and any alteration in the speed or regularity of the movement.

But the time will soon come when the rider's descent of the hand and descent of the leg are complete and long. So it is that the horse soon learns to carry himself.

V.   THE *RASSEMBLER*

The *rassembler* is accomplished without the horse advancing in any noticeable fashion. It consists of provoking the functioning, the putting into play, of the *ressorts* (springs, joints, resources) of the horse's body to obtain "action" in place, or if the horse is in movement, of augmenting the action or the movement without causing an appreciable increase in speed.

It has as a result the engagement of the hind legs under the body and the elevation of the movement (action).

What the *rassembler* produces. – Therefore it is the rassembler that causes the horse to sit down (on his hocks), to diminish his base of support, and give height to the various gaits.

A complete rassembler is possible only in place. It takes the name piaffe (*piaffer*) when it is done with rhythm, measure, and cadence.

It is not indispensable to go all the way to piaffe. But a horse is not truly *dressé* (dressed, straightened, trained) if the rider does not have the *rassembler* at his disposal to sit the horse down at divers gaits, and thus make him more agreeable, more secure, and more brilliant.

How to ask for the *rassembler*. - The horse should always be light and in ramener before the rider tries for the *rassembler*. In order to make the horse better understand the aids for the *rassembler*, it is good to begin this instruction in hand by means of the whip and then later return to this elementary procedure even though it is not a *sine qua non* condition of success.

But whether in hand or mounted, the rider must be content with little at the beginning.

Since in these exercises the horse has a tendency to come back on himself, to back up more or less, it is indispensable to push him softly forward with the leg, or if necessary, by a gradual and progressive pressure of the spurs, and later by little *attaques* of the spur *each time that the rider asks for the rassembler in place* and before the horse stops himself.

The hand, which has been softly fixed while the leg aids demanded mobility, gives (the reins) slightly at the moment when the legs increase their pressure. Then, right away, the hand receives the increased impulsion and takes over skillfully (from the legs) to confirm the lightness that has been more or less compromised.

The rider then stops, and finishes by re-establishing calm and balance before starting again.

It is also necessary to exercise the horse in *rassembler* at different gaits.

For that, the rider's legs progressively activate the horse; the hand keeps the horse from increasing his speed, and the growth in action thus obtained brings the engagement of the hind legs under the mass and a greater elevation in the movement.

It would do well to discuss the difference between the

rassembler and the *effet d'ensemble*.

The purpose of the *effet d'ensemble*. - The purpose of the *effet d'ensemble* is to immobilize the horse, or to force him to hold the gait and direction desired.

To accomplish the *effet d'ensemble*, the rider must use the hand, legs, and, if needed, spurs *with a continuous and graduated progression* until the desired effect is obtained.

On the contrary, in the *rassembler*, it is the mobility of the extremities or a greater thrust of the *ressorts* (springs, joints, resources) that the rider endeavors to produce and maintain. So the legs, and if necessary the spurs, must make themselves felt *by successive, repeated, alternating even, but not continuous* pressure.

Summing up, the *effet d'ensemble* calms, extinguishes, or regulates; the *rassembler* animates, revives, and excites activity, giving life and brilliance.

PROGRESSION OF DRESSAGE

In dressage one wants always to go too quickly.
To succeed promptly, do not hurry, but solidly assure each step.
Ask often; be content with little; reward generously.
The lesson must be, for the horse as well as for the rider,
A salutary exercise, an instructive play that never brings fatigue.
When sweat appears, the rider has gone too far.

PART ONE: PREPARATION

CHAPTER I : FLEXIONS-WORK WITH THE WHIP,

USE OF THE LUNGE WHIP

The horse is bridled, but without a saddle. He wears a cavesson to which an aide attaches a longe line and maintains it in half-tension. But it can be removed as soon as possible. There are even many horses for which it may be dispensed with entirely. During the work in hand, remove the curb chain from time to time to have more mobility of the jaw, and repeat the different movements with it off.

Three ways to work with the bridoon and the curb. - There are three ways to use the bridoon reins or those of the curb.

The first is that which everyone uses to give direction.

The second is the half-halt. It is with this action that the rider fights against *weight*.

If while feeling the mouth, by acting on the corners of the lips using the bridoon to request lightness, the rider meets the force of inertia, that blunt force that makes weight keep the horse from raising his neck and chewing softly to yield to the bit, then give him a half-halt; that is, rapidly and progressively at the first feeling of resistance, without stopping to rest in contact with the mouth, increase the pressure. Then give (the reins); take again; give a second half-halt, then a third, etc. as necessary until the horse yields his jaw.

The third is the vibration, a little trembling produced by nimbly agitating the hand.

This action combats the *forces* with which the horse resists when the rider feels the horse's mouth, where instead of yielding his jaw, he contracts it voluntarily in order to resist. The rider gives (the reins) and then begins again, if required.

The rider must not look to give direction until the horse is light; that is, in balance, when the rider no longer has to fight against the weight nor the forces.

Lift the neck as much as possible. - The rider, taking the whip with the point lowered, places himself in front of the horse and looks at him. He takes a bridoon rein in each hand near the bit and lifts the head and neck as much as possible by extending his arms.

The rider is looking, in this way, for some appearance of lightness. After a minute of rest, during which he keeps the neck from lowering, he starts over with the same effect on the curb. When he has obtained lightness, he lets the horse free so that he remains left to himself as much as possible, whether at the halt, at the walk, or the rein-back. The horse must learn early to hold his head himself, and to guard its position.

But when the head moves, take back the horse.

Walk forward on the whip. - Then, taking both curb reins in his left hand near the bit, the rider holds the whip in his other hand, horizontally, so as to point to the horse's middle without touching him with the lash. Then he lightly touches the chest in gentle upward strokes, repeated at one second intervals until the horse makes a step forward.

If the horse resists or looks to charge forward, the rider may punish him with the cavesson (or the bit).

If the horse moves backwards or throws himself to one side, the rider limits himself to continuing the light touches of the whip without letting go of an energetic tension on the reins.

Be content with obtaining one step, very straight, with the neck held up.

Caress the front of the horse's head and let him rest for one or two minutes before beginning again. Then, ask for two steps, then three, etc. Should the horse traverse himself in the least, *stop*. Put him back to perfectly straight, by the shoulders principally, and then ask for the walk again. Continue until he will step forward brightly on the very *approach* of the whip.

Then move to rein-back.

Rein-back. - The rider, hands high, faces the horse, and to start, places him perfectly straight in the shoulders and the haunches, and requests a little lightness.

Then holding one bridoon rein in each hand, he lifts his arms again acting on the corners of the lips upwards (and

slightly backwards) in a manner to bring about the rein-back by the shifting of weight onto the hindquarters.

"Forcer le mouvement." - If at a soft indication of the reins, the backward step is not produced, it is necessary to

"forcer le mouvement" ; that is, the rider must *progressively* increase the effect of the bit so that the horse feels it with an intensity growing almost imperceptibly, but energetically, until the movement to the rear, the rein-back, is obtained. The tact consists in stopping the effect in question at the precise instant when the resistance yields and the horse carries his hindquarters to the rear, if only for several centimeters.

The horse must not rein back but a step, but perfectly straight; that is the most important objective. If the croup carries itself to one side or the other, straighten the horse immediately by the shoulders, mobilized toward the right or left, as the case may be, to oppose the haunches.

Afterwards, make him do the same exercise using the curb reins in the same manner as for the bridoon.

Flexions. - Next we move on to flexions. They are divided into two types:

1ST: The direct flexion of the jaw, which is made by acting on, at the same time, both of the bridoon reins, or those of the curb.

2ND: The semi-lateral flexion of the jaw and neck, which is asked for on each rein separately.

Before seeking these flexions directly, as we will want to do shortly, we will make five other flexions that are only to prepare the horse. We will not be using them later, but, since in principle they are easily obtained, the horse will understand more quickly, by this means, what we want him to do; furthermore, their use makes the rider more skillful with the reins.

The *goal* of any flexion is *to obtain lightness*, such as it has been defined above.

Preparatory flexions.

A. *With the two curb reins.* For the first preparatory flexion, the rider places himself, to start, to the left of the horse beside the forward extremity of the neck (facing forward). He takes the right curb rein in the right hand (under the neck) sixteen centimeters from the bit, and the left rein (in the left hand) at only ten centimeters. Then he lifts the horse's head as much as possible and lightly and progressively brings his right hand towards his body while extending his left. If this effect, continued for several seconds, does not bring about lightness, he employs a half-halt or a vibration, as the case may be, but he applies them on the left rein. When the jaw is softly mobilized, he gives (the reins).

Then the rider places himself to the right of the horse, asks for the same flexion by the inverse means, acting on the left bar (of the jaw).

B. *With the two bridoon reins.* The rider moves on to the second preparatory flexion.

He comes back to the near side facing forward, and after lifting the neck, crosses the bridoon reins under the jaw, the left rein in the right hand, and the right rein in the left hand, sixteen centimeters from the bit.

He asks for lightness by creating an equal and progressive traction on both reins at the same time, and gives (the reins) when lightness is manifested.

C. *With a bridoon rein and a curb rein on the same side.* - The third preparatory flexion is again started on the left (but close to the head and facing the eye, not the

forehead). The rider takes the left bridoon rein in the left hand and the left curb rein in the right hand. He lifts the head and neck and then provokes a separation of the jaws by carrying the left hand sideways toward the front of the horse and the right hand toward the left shoulder. If he has to vanquish some resistance, he gives the half-halts or vibrations on the bridoon only. When the jaw is mobilized, he gives (the reins).

He repeats this flexion on the right by moving to the right side and making the same request with the other reins.

D. *With the two bridoon reins, to obtain an eighth of a flexion of the neck.* - For the fourth preparatory flexion, the rider places himself near the left shoulder. He takes the off-side bridoon rein in his right hand and holds it while pressing on the base of the neck. (The right rein passes over the neck to the base of the neck on the left side. See the fifth (E) preparatory flexion below. See also F. Baucher, *New Method of Horsemanship*, 9th edition, in Hilda Nelson, *François Baucher, The Man and his Method*, Xenophon Press 2013, and Dominic Olivier, *Equitation: Flexions et Dressage à Pied*, Chiron, Paris 1997.)The other bridoon rein is held with the left hand, thirty centimeters from the bit. As usual, it serves at first to lift the head as high as possible.

As soon as lightness comes, while the head is inclined a little to the right so as to produce an eighth of a flexion of the neck, the rider hastens to give (the reins).

When necessary, the half-halts or vibrations are given here on the left rein.

The rider repeats the flexion standing on the right side and asking in an analogous manner for the jaw and neck to yield to the left.

E. *With the two curb reins, one of them passing over the neck.* - Finally, the rider obtains the fifth preparatory flexion by placing himself at the left and taking the curb reins as he did those of the bridoon in the fourth preparatory flexion.

After having lifted the neck as much as possible, he takes an equal half-tension on both reins so as to obtain lightness by acting on both branches of the curb at the same time.

In all the preparatory flexions, the rider must ensure that the horse's head remains high with the neck very steady.

The rider opposes the resistances that are instinctive to the horse by half-halts. That is how he avoids fights.

As soon as the head lowers or turns, again use half-halts until the horse remains immobile, or the rider places his head for him.

We might remark that it is not useful for the horse to open his mouth during flexions. It suffices that he makes his bits "jump" (with his tongue) and softly mobilizes his lower jaw.

It is even preferable that the separation of the jaws be hardly apparent. But the head must not move after the flexion of the jaw.

When the horse executes these five preparatory flexions easily, the rider moves on to the two flexions of which we have spoken above, and that should be asked for only after the preparatory flexions.

Direct flexions of the jaw. – 1st-For the direct flexion of the jaw, the rider places himself in front of the horse with a bridoon rein in each hand and begins by lifting the neck and head as much as possible, using half-halts as necessary; then, he asks for lightness with an equal and continuous half-tension on both reins upward and backward in a manner that the bit acts only on the corners of the lips (taking care that the horse does not move backwards).

If after several seconds this slow force does not bring lightness, the rider employs a half-halt or a vibration according to the circumstance. Then he feels the mouth again. If this new soft contact does not bring lightness, he again uses the same effects until it is obtained. Afterwards, this same flexion is repeated with the curb reins.

Semi-lateral flexions of the jaw and the neck. - Then: 2nd- The rider moves to the semi-lateral flexions of the jaw and the neck.

At first the rider asks for lightness on the bridoon, as in the preceding case. Then he acts on one rein only in a manner so as to obtain, by pressure on the corresponding corner of the lips, a lateral movement of the head that produces the beginning of a flexion of the neck; finally, he completes the effect by perfecting lightness on the same rein. When this result is obtained, the flexion has been made. The rider repeats the exercise on the other bridoon rein, and then, according to the same principles, on each curb rein.

When making these flexions, the rider should take care to let the horse rest by releasing the reins completely for one or two minutes each time that the horse is very light. He should also in this way teach the horse to support himself. The rider can punish the horse with half-halts when he moves his head or lowers his neck.

The rider goes on to make the same two flexions again by taking direct hold of the rings of the bridoon and then the branches of the curb.

Return to the walk on the whip, and to the rein-back. When the horse understands the flexions well, the rider must return to the walk on the whip and to the rein-back in order to perfect these two exercises.

From this moment on, the rider, before trying anything else, insists on complete lightness.

He watches that lightness remains unchanged during the walk or the rein-back. The horse should remain perfectly straight and move only calmly and slowly. The rider leaves the horse at liberty as much as possible so that he becomes accustomed to conserving his balance without tension and continuing his movement by himself with the regularity of a pendulum.

The rider stops each time that the regularity he had obtained is altered.

Then, before starting again, he accords the horse several seconds of complete rest and then re-establishes balance by achieving lightness again.

Afterwards, the rider begins *pas de coté* (steps to the side, lateral movements), *pirouettes renversées* (reversed pirouettes, turns on the forehand), and *pirouettes ordinaires* (ordinary pirouettes, turns on the haunches).

For each of these exercises, the horse first must be light, calm, *décontracté* (de-contracted, relaxed), and perfectly straight. Then the rider, taking the curb reins in the left hand, requests the movement, which will in turn provoke a muscular contraction. As soon as a step is obtained, the rider halts to relax (the jaw) again, before requesting another step.

Steps to the side (Lateral movements). - For the lateral movements, the rider positions the forehand in the direction of the movement and makes the croup follow by showing the horse the whip. He may tap the horse several times, as needed.

If a very strong resistance in the croup is manifested, the rider will triumph by opposition of the hand, which he stops immediately when the yielding of the croup is obtained. The horse's shoulders must well precede his haunches, and each left leg, if the rider is applying pressure from left to right, for example, must pass in front of its neighbor on the off side.

Finally, the horse must not advance (the shoulders must not get so far in front of the croup that the horse loses the proper lateral movement even though remaining on a diagonal path).

Reversed pirouettes (Turns on the forehand). - In the turn on the forehand, from left to right, for example, the near fore leg must not leave the ground.

The rider places himself at the left shoulder and menaces the left flank, which he can tap lightly if necessary.

Ordinary pirouettes (Turns on the haunches). – Finally, we come to the ordinary pirouette. For it to be performed correctly, from left to right, for example, the right hind leg must serve as a pivot and remain fixed to the ground. The left fore must pass in front of the right fore. If it passes behind, the horse has come back on himself.

The rider sets himself up with the whip in a manner to impede the sideways movement of the croup as needed.

The rider continues this work, seeking every day to come closer to perfection; he must come to the point at which the horse obeys a simple gesture without needing to be touched and executes each of his movements while remaining in balance.

Requesting this preparatory work with a simple gesture. - The horse, once rendered light, must begin the walk on the whip, the steps to the side, or the pirouettes, *before contact with the whip* while it is still a little away from the hair of his coat. Similarly, once lightness is obtained, the rein-back must begin when the rider steps slowly toward the horse while looking at him, both hands raised and very near the bit, but before he touches it.

Of course, the rein-back must be executed with the greatest calm and regularity, without the horse making the next step until the rider requests it.

The perfection that we have described is the goal towards which the instruction of the horse must be directed. But it is only later, when the mounted work has begun, that the rider can hope to achieve this goal.

So it is enough that the horse understands the mechanics of the preceding movements and that he execute the flexions well for the rider to have him mounted by an aide.

Furthermore, it is preferable to not begin the *rassembler*, even in hand, until the rider has already obtained the ramener mounted, at the walk and at the *petit trot* (small trot, collected trot).

***Rassembler*. - First habituate the horse to the longe whip**. - With the horse on the track on the left hand, the rider holds the lowered longe whip in the right hand, and, in the other, the curb reins near the bit.

He fixes his gaze on the eyes of the horse and requests lightness. Then he slowly lifts the longe whip. But should the horse move, the rider stops, holding his arm still until he has immobilized the horse with half-halts and a severe expression while still looking into his eyes.

As soon as immobility is obtained, the rider reassures the horse with the interjection: "Ohh!" uttered in a caressing voice.

The rider progresses to placing the lanyard of the whip firmly on the horse, with the lash hanging over the off side, the end of the shaft applied to the left side of the back.

If, at this contact, the horse appears uneasy, the rider immobilizes him with the left hand, as we have described above, while leaving the longe whip lightly on the horse's back.

When calm is restored, the rider slides the whip backwards so that the end of the shaft comes a little past the left haunch. Then, he lowers it until it touches the ground in such a manner that the lanyard passes softly over the croup.

How to accustom the horse to the noise of the lash, or to any fearsome object, or to have him shod, etc. - Before going farther, let us say that it is by a similar procedure that the fearful horse is accustomed to the noise of the lash: first, on the track on both hands and then in the middle of the school.

The rider shakes the lash quietly near the ground while fixing his eyes with benevolence on those of the horse, whom he immobilizes the way we have described above when the horse is disturbed.

When the horse shows calm, the rider caresses him, and then agitates the lash more vividly.

He should get to the point where he can crack the whip near the ear of a reassured and tranquil horse.

The rider's gaze is of extreme importance in all of these practices.

It is by a similar progression that a rider can accustom the most savage and the most ferocious characters to any object that frightens them and bring the most irascible and malicious horses to be shod without difficulty.

Starting the *rassembler* with the longe whip on the track. - When the horse remains calm and immobile under the longe whip, the rider can ask for the *rassembler*.

For this, he looks for lightness first. Then, he shakes the longe whip near the left haunch while clicking his tongue. He touches the horse as needed with the shaft or the lanyard, but as little as possible, so as to avoid exasperating the horse and causing a fight.

As soon as the horse mobilizes his legs, but before he advances, the rider places the longe whip, as we have explained above, on the horse's back, and slides it down to the ground by way of the croup. Using half-halts, the rider should stop the horse *before he stops himself.*

The rider starts over again several times, taking care to make the horse walk a step or two after each iteration of *rassembler* so that he does not stay too long in the same place while lifting his legs, but rather advances a little.

Starting the *rassembler* with the whip on the track. - When the horse well understands this work, the rider, still on the track, tries the *rassembler* with the whip, which he holds as for the longe whip, and shows it near the flank. He only touches the horse if clicks of the tongue and the threat of the whip are impotent.

To stop the horse, the rider at first lays the whip, softly but firmly, diagonally on the back (pointed toward the croup, while half-halting). But later, the half-halts should suffice.

These first requests for the *rassembler* made on the track are only to make the horse more easily understand what the rider wants of him.

As soon as possible, the rider should try the *rassembler* in the middle of the school, first with the longe whip, then later with the whip.

On the track, the wall prevents the rider from having "the complete ensemble of the forces of the horse." So, it will go better if the rider believes himself skillful enough to start on the first day in the middle of the school, as we are going to explain.

Rassembler in the middle of the school with the longe whip. - The rider holds the curb reins in the left hand near the bit and the longe whip in the right hand.

He begins by repeating the work that he did on the track to habituate the horse to calming himself and to halting at the contact of the longe whip. Having made the horse light, he asks for the *rassembler* by lifting the lash above the croup.

If the horse steps sideways, the rider displays the longe whip either on the right or on the left by passing the lash behind the horse, always bringing the longe whip back to its elevated position above the croup. He touches the hindquarters when necessary but still as rarely as possible.

Imperceptibly, he comes to leave the longe whip at the side of the horse, even quite low, but when the action dies out, he lifts it and uses it delicately.

As soon as he obtains the slight beginning of mobility of the legs in place, with the horse remaining perfectly straight, and neither advancing nor backing up, he stops the horse right away by an enveloping contact with the

lunge whip; then, he *relaxes* completely and allows several seconds of rest before starting again.

Beginning with these first lessons, the rider must try to teach the horse to collect himself without aids. He must try to start the action of the horse without touching him and without using his hand to impede the weight from falling on the forehand.

Rassembler in the middle of the school with the whip. - When the *rassembler* has been executed thus without difficulties, the rider can request it with the whip, which he holds in place of the longe whip in the right hand.

He starts, as always, with lightness. Then he displays the whip (raising the lowered point toward the flank) several times to create the action.

The rider then lifts the whip to (rest on) top of the back of the horse, which he calms with his voice, and asks for the halt with light effects of the hand.

Repeat several times changing hands.

Once the horse is perfectly tranquil and perfectly straight under the whip, the rider can excite him to the *rassembler* by a click of the tongue, and, if needed, by touching him delicately with the lash on the croup.

As soon as the horse mobilizes himself in place, the rider stops him, *relaxes,* and begins again.

If the horse kicks, the rider corrects him with the hand that holds the reins, but never with the whip.

It is important to pay the greatest attention that the horse not have his weight balanced on the forehand in the *rassembler*. Also, before requesting the *rassembler*, it is absolutely necessary to relieve the forehand; that is to obtain lightness with the elevation of the neck.

The rider should endeavor to arrive at the mobilization of the horse's legs without the hand being necessary to prohibit the horse from advancing and without the whip being felt.

Finally, if the horse is not perfectly straight, he must be stopped immediately, re-straightened, and *relaxed* before starting again. This is of the highest importance.

In the middle of a square cornered school, it is convenient to line the horse up with the walls to make sure that the horse is, and remains, straight in the shoulders and the haunches.

Important recommendations. - During the *rassembler*, the hind legs advance under the horse's body, but the rider need not demand that they remain engaged when their action ceases.

The rider must pay great attention, from the beginning, that he makes both hind legs engage equally.

It often happens that one of the diagonal pairs of legs, the left for example, comes down a little behind the other. This is especially true for the hind leg of the diagonal pair, the right hind in this example. This should not be allowed to continue too long. So, while he is producing the *rassembler*, the rider makes the horse advance a little and he tries, by skillful effects of the hand and the whip, to bring the two legs into line.

The rider should not hold such a horse perfectly straight, but rather, in this example, see that the croup is carried a little to the left, without exaggeration, in order to bring out more activity in the right hind.

It is very important to correct, in this way, the fault of which we speak, because once the rider lets a horse take on this bad habit, it is nearly impossible to make him lose it.

The work in hand being but a preparation for what we propose to request later in the saddle, the rider should not sacrifice the principal for the accessory.

So, the rider should hasten to have an aide mount the horse that he is training.

But nonetheless, he should continue the work in hand each day in order to render the *rassembler* closer to perfection. While doing so, he should look unceasingly to obtain the *rassembler* with the most constant lightness and regularity.

From that constant lightness and regularity, the *rassembler* itself will produce rhythm and so become the piaffe.

CHAPTER II THE EQUITATION OF FANTASY

-ARTIFICIAL GAITS (AIRS)

Piaffe. - With the piaffe, we can enter the equitation of fantasy, learned equitation, full of enjoyment, useful even to perfect the horse, but not required for ordinary training.

When the piaffe is done correctly, the steps are separated more and more in time, and are more elevated at each lesson.

The horse should continue to cadence himself with no hand, nor clicks of the tongue, nor whip, but always perfectly straight, the neck well supported with constant lightness, and without advancing or backing up.

If the forelegs are not elevated as much as the hind, the rider should touch the horse's chest with the whip. If the horse wants to stamp with his hind legs, the rider may prevent that by half-halts. If this means does not suffice, he can go back to using the cavesson.

If the hind end lacks activity, the rider should from time to time tap sharply on the croup.

Passage. Trot to the rear. - Next, the rider exercises the horse in piaffe, letting him advance three or four centimeters to start, then ten or fifteen centimeters each time. This constitutes the *passage,* and similarly reining back an inch or two at each step in cadence is called *trot to the rear*.

These two airs increase in beauty as the horse gains less ground forward or to the rear, and as the support phase of each diagonal pair of legs is more elevated and prolonged, with lightness remaining intact.

The rider asks for all of this work by the whip, but can sometimes use the longe whip with equal effectiveness.

It is not always necessary to unsaddle the horse. When the horse remains saddled, tapping the whip on the seat of the saddle will suffice to excite him. Touching the croup should be used only as an extreme means.

Complete horizontal extension of each foreleg by means of the whip. - When each of the preceding movements in work in hand is well understood by the horse, the rider can begin to make the horse lift his forelegs alternatively on the whip aid.

For this exercise, the rider places himself in front of the horse, whose head he has lifted with his left hand, and assures himself that the horse is light. In the other hand, he holds the whip, point lowered.

At one second intervals, he taps lightly the forearm of the leg that he wants lifted until the horse lifts his leg, even if only slightly. The hand that holds the reins lightens the same side by making the horse's weight shift onto the other foot, which stays on the ground.

The rider corrects any movement caused by irate behavior of the horse by half-halts, and he re-straightens the horse using the whip with which he stopped tapping the horse's forearm as soon as immobility of his body and his calm disappeared. According to principle, the rider rewards the horse as soon as the foot is detached from the ground, even if only for an instant. Next, he performs the same procedure to lift the other foot.

As this exercise becomes more familiar to the horse, the rider asks for more and more suspension, extension, and elevation of each leg; that is, he stops the taps of the whip only when he has obtained progress, even if hardly appreciable, compared to what the horse had produced previously. In addition, the rider must assure himself that the lightness has not at all been altered.

Acting as above with a great deal of tact while increasing his demands only imperceptibly, the rider will achieve the complete extension of each foreleg held horizontally for as long as he does not permit it to be lowered.

Spanish walk. - Now it is time to begin the *Spanish walk*.

To obtain this air, the rider starts by putting the horse on the track on the left hand. He holds the reins and the whip as before, but he places himself a little to the inside of the school, so as to not be hit by the forelegs. Then he requests lightness, and then the lifting of one of the forelegs.

During the extension of the leg, he touches the horse on the chest with the whip to provoke a step forward.

The step having been executed, the rider stops, re-establishes the balance if it has been lost, then he makes the horse raise the other leg.

He immediately asks for another step, then a halt. Then, he checks the lightness, and so on.

The rider restarts the exercise on the other hand, placing himself by the horse in an analogous manner.

As soon as this walk is understood by the horse, the rider tries to obtain it from this point onward with the least possible use of the whip, shifting the weight alternatively on to the leg resting on the ground, while the other leg is extended as far as it is capable during its suspension.

The rider moves away as soon as possible from the track, not to return, and he strives, day by day, to arrive at a state of unchanging lightness, the horse easily taking up this artificial gait which should be cadenced, harmonious, and as slow as the rider wants it.

Spanish trot. - The rider moves next to the *Spanish trot*.

For this, he starts again on the track. But the rider should place himself beside the horse facing forward so that he is not obliged to walk backwards. If he is on the left hand, for example, he holds the curb reins in the right hand and the whip in the other.

The rider puts the horse at the Spanish walk, then, facilitating the gait by alternately displacing of the weight toward the right and toward the left, he increases the horse's speed by tapping lightly on the chest with the whip as needed. Similarly, he can by touching the forearms maintain the extension or elevation of the legs as necessary.

The rider constantly watches the lightness.

As the horse becomes accustomed to a more rapid beat in the Spanish walk, the rider accelerates the beat more and more, imperceptibly, in a manner to obtain the birth of the trot, which is produced, as we know, when the strides of the walk, after being brought more and more together, finish by joining two by two diagonally.

As soon as he has achieved one or two strides of trot with the extension of the forelegs, the rider stops, he *relaxes*, and then starts again.

These trials are repeated on the right hand according to the same principles.

The rider should move away from the track as soon as possible. The requirement is, by requesting each day one or two more strides before stopping, by progressively coming to the point where it suffices to show the whip and to shift the weight from one shoulder to the other, that the Spanish trot be produced with great elevation, with lightness remaining intact, with the legs completely extended horizontally, with the steps being produced at long and equal intervals, and with each diagonal pair of legs passing from support to suspension from a soft and elastic thrust that makes the horse advance only a little.

A horse can be otherwise perfectly balanced and completely dressed (trained and straightened) without the Spanish trot or walk, and without even learning to lift his forelegs at the will of the rider.

So these different exercises are not at all an indispensable part of dressage, and one can, without inconvenience, abstain from asking for them.

But from another point of view, the Spanish trot is the most powerful means for the greatest development of movement in the horse's shoulders.

Sustained extended trot. - When a horse can take this artificial gait easily, the rider can look, little by little, to accelerate the tempo without altering the brilliant horizontal projection of the forelegs, and come then to the *extended trot with sustained suspension.*

But it is above all when mounted that this trot can be taught by the rider, and obtained in all its beauty.

CHAPTER III THE FIRST LESSON IN MOUNTING

The horse is saddled

Dominate the horse. Reward him as soon as he shows submission. Proceed extremely gradually.

If the rider (trainer) has a horse that he does not trust, whether it is because the horse has never carried a rider, or because the horse has shown a ferocious or crotchety character, he should put a cavesson on the horse and hold it with a longe line.

To start, the rider places himself on the track on the left hand. He makes the horse walk by use of the whip. After several steps, he stops the horse with a *saccade* (a more or less gentle tug upward) on the cavesson using moderate force but sufficient to make the horse understand the power of the instrument that he has on his nose.

The rider again asks for the walk on the whip, then he again halts, but by a light *saccade* on the cavesson.

When the horse seems to feel a salutary fear of the cavesson, and shows himself acceptably submissive to the rider, an aide approaches and places himself at the left shoulder. The rider strokes the horse on the neck and looks at him with benevolence.

The aide takes the bridoon reins crossed in his left hand, together with taking hold of the mane in the same hand, and pulls them toward himself.

If the horse moves, the aide stops all action and stays at the shoulder. The rider gives a *saccade* on the cavesson proportioned to the fault and straightens the horse.

Calm re-established, the aide starts again.

If the horse remains immobile, the rider flatters him with a look, with his hand, and his voice. The aide stops pulling the mane and strokes the horse on the neck. When the horse allows this action quietly, the aide takes the left stirrup leather and slaps it against the saddle. The rider acts as explained above, according to whether the horse frets or remains calm.

Then the aide puts his foot in the stirrup, but removes it very quickly if the immobility disappears. Then, he lifts himself very slowly; avoiding touching the horse with the point of his foot, caresses the back and the croup, and then immediately lowers himself to the ground without being abrupt.

The aide begins again, lifting himself on the stirrup, and finally passes his right leg over the back to arrive gently in the saddle. If at that moment the horse shows worry or alarm, the aide jumps to the ground with his best agility.

During all this series of progressive actions, the rider, holding the cavesson, is extra careful, encourages the submission of the horse, flatters him with his voice and right hand, but punishes any manifestation of revolt or impatience by vertical *saccades*, but giving only one *saccade* per fault.

Calm appearing complete; the aide begins again to put himself in the saddle. Then he puts his right foot in the stirrup. After that, he leaves the saddle delicately, passing his right leg back over the croup, stops for a moment on the left stirrup, caresses the horse again with the right hand, and drops softly to the ground.

The rider then makes the horse walk several steps forward on the whip while flattering him so as to augment the horse's confidence and to reclaim his attention.

When this procedure has been repeated several times, the rider directs the aide, already in the saddle and having both feet in the stirrups, to separate the bridoon reins and to settle his seat. Then, the rider makes the horse walk on the whip.

If the depart is calm and regular, he flatters the horse with his voice and gaze while caressing the horse's neck.

If it is otherwise, the fault is immediately punished by an appropriate *saccade* on the cavesson and then the rider (trainer, not the aide) re-establishes confidence and starts again until the first step is good.

Next, they stop, and the aide dismounts. They continue this lesson on the track until the lesson is well understood. Then, they repeat it in the middle of the school as often as necessary.

Then, the rider removes the cavesson, and puts the horse back on the track on the left hand, the rider still on foot and holding the curb reins near the bit in the left hand so that he can make half-halts if he needs to correct the horse.

When the horse allows himself to be mounted (by the aide) without moving on the track and without the rider using the cavesson, the rider puts the horse in the middle of the school.

When, in the middle of the school, the aide can get into the saddle without the horse appearing alarmed, and the depart to the walk on the whip is regular and calm, the rider may dismiss the aide and ride the horse himself.

To this end, he again puts the horse on the track as previously. He takes the end of the curb reins in his right hand and repeats the lesson as we have described it, with this difference; he will correct all of the horse's faults with half-halts on the curb, and, once in the saddle, will not ask the horse to walk.

If the horse backs up at his approach (before he mounts), the rider comes back to the horse's chest, without being abrupt, and makes him advance on the whip as often as necessary. (In mounting) the rider must keep his right hand as free as possible, not using it to lift himself, nor hold himself, except when he cannot do otherwise. He must redouble his tact and skill.

With the lesson well understood on the track, it is given again in the middle of the school. When the horse remains calm and immobile then, one can pronounce him "confirmed to be mounted."

If, by reason of the history of the horse, or of his mild and submissive character, the rider judges it useless in principle to employ the cavesson, the lesson (in mounting) can be given with the bridle only, in the same manner and carefully following the same progression, with this difference; the rider, working in hand, corrects with half-halts all the rebellious movements of the horse, both instinctive and voluntary.

CHAPTER IV REPEATING THE WORK TAUGHT IN HAND WITH AN AIDE IN THE SADDLE. THE LESSON OF THE SPUR

The rider (trainer) has an aide mount the horse, fitted with a cavesson, unless the rider judges, for serious reasons, that this precaution will not be useful.

The lesson is given from the beginning in the middle of the school.

The rider, working in hand, holds the longe line attached to the cavesson, or if he has not fitted the cavesson, holds the curb reins near the bit.

The aide takes a bridoon rein in each hand and occupies himself, at first, with only his seat, leaving himself to be carried without acting at all on the horse.

The rider, still working in hand, then asks for all the same work that has been learned up until now unmounted. This is to familiarize the horse with the weight of the rider.

When each of these exercises is easily executed, the rider instructs the aide to request them from the saddle.

The aide begins with the flexions.

Flexions. - The aide therefore begins with lightness on both bridoon reins at the same time, with the head and neck well elevated.

He then requests lightness on both curb reins, then on each bridoon rein and each curb rein separately, always alternating them as is prescribed.

Walk. - Once the flexions are accomplished, the aide closes both his legs equally and progressively.

If the horse carries himself forward on this effect, the legs are relaxed; they caress the horse and stop him. Straight away, the aide asks for lightness again.

If, at the approach of the aide's leg, the horse does not carry himself forward, the rider, working in hand, directs him to obey the legs by the whip at the chest, in order to make him understand what they want at the touch of the calves. They repeat this exercise until the contact of the pant leg or the boot produces the walk forward.

Rein-back. Steps to the side. Pirouettes, Beginning the *rassembler* **(and the Spanish walk).** - Using the same principles, the aide requests the rein-back, the steps to the side (lateral movements), the pirouettes, then, on the track on both hands, some suspicion of the *rassembler* (*and even a little Spanish walk*), if the horse has already been sufficiently prepared.

As we have already explained for the walk forward, the rider pays attention to making the horse understand what he wants of him when he shows the least hesitation.

The rider and the aide content themselves with the slightest appearance of obedience, reward the horse very quickly, and then give him a rest.

If the horse puts up any defense or commits whatever fault, the cavesson acts immediately as a punishment.

If the rider has believed himself sure enough of the horse that he has undertaken not to put this instrument on the horse, then, working in hand, he contents himself to hold the curb reins steadily, close to the bit; but it is still he- and not the aide on the horse-who corrects the horse with half-halts each time that it is necessary.

These same prescriptions apply to the lesson that we are about to detail, and that has as its goal to teach the horse to know the spur.

The rider may give this lesson when the horse begins to respond to the aids of the man who is mounted on him.

Habituating the horse to the spur. - Here is how the rider should proceed.

Applying the calves. - With the aide wearing boots without spurs, the rider directs him, after he has obtained good lightness using both bridoon reins, to approach the horse's flanks with both of his calves and to increase the pressure slowly, while holding (not pulling) the bridoon in opposition sufficient to prevent the horse from carrying himself forward.

If the horse conserves his immobility, his calm, and his lightness while the aide tightens his legs with certain energy, both the rider and the aide hasten to give (the reins) completely and caress the horse.

If he moves or frets, the aide continues the pressure of his calves without increasing it, and the rider acts with *saccades* on the cavesson, or by half-halts on the curb, until immobility returns. Then the aide releases his legs very quickly, and the rider flatters the horse with his voice and his hand.

Applying the heel-no spur. - When the horse supports the strongest pressure of the legs of the aide, losing not his calm, nor his immobility, nor his lightness, the rider instructs the aide to close his legs down to the contact of the heels.

When a strong application of the heels without spurs is accepted with the same tranquility as with the calves, the rider puts spurs on the aide's boots. But he takes care to wrap the rowels with little pieces of linen or cotton cloth enclosed in pieces of leather, or the ends of the fingers of a glove tied with strings around the shafts of the spurs.

Applying the covered rowels. - The rider and his aide follow the same procedure as the preceding to habituate the horse to the covered rowels.

Applying the uncovered rowels. - The rider removes all the covering from the aide's spurs, and again starts the same procedures as used for the application of the calves, the bare heels, and the covered spurs, acting with yet more delicacy, if possible.

At the halt. - So in the same way, the rider and the aide start by having the aide squeeze his calves with great energy. Then the spur approaches progressively to the hair of the coat, where it presses *frankly*, but with not with too much power to start.

When he has made contact with the spur, at the first moment of calm, immobility, and lightness, the aide hastens to give (the reins); in this case he lowers his hands, and loosens his legs completely, starting by taking his spurs away from the horse's flank, and lastly by releasing his calves. The rider and the aide caress the horse at the same time.

If the horse "kicks at the boot," the rider, working in hand, punishes him with the cavesson or with half-halts on the curb.

They repeat often this approach of the spur at the halt, showing great generosity in rewarding the horse in a manner to confirm him well in this exercise and to make him understand well that what they are looking for is immobility and lightness and that they will flatter him as soon as he is calm and tranquil.

Walk forward on the spur. When this result has been achieved, it is necessary afterward and *of the utmost importance* to habituate the horse to "carry himself from the halt forward on the spur."

To ensure this effect, the aide holds the spurs at the hair of the horse's coat while holding the reins in opposition to maintain immobility. When the horse becomes light, the aide lowers his hands a little and increases the pressure of the spur.

If the horse carries himself forward, the spur aids release immediately, and then the hand stops (the horse).

The rider and his aide repeat the exercise many times.

If the horse does not walk a step by the time the pressure of the spur has attained its maximum intensity, the rider, working in hand, directs the horse to carry himself forward by touching the horse on the chest with the whip.

They repeat this exercise as often as necessary to confirm the horse well in it.

Applying the spur while walking. Then with the aide riding the horse at the walk, the rider tells him first to apply the calves, then to softly but *frankly* apply the spur, with the aide's hand preventing the acceleration of the pace; the aide must avoid a timid approach of the spur that produces intermittent contact, which tickles or irritates the horse.

If the arrival of the spur at the hair of the coat brings on disorder, the rider, still working in hand, re-establishes calm and the regularity of the walk by the cavesson, or by half-halts on the curb.

Going from walk to trot on the spur. - Now it is necessary to accustom the horse, with the spur at the hair of the coat, to go from walk to trot by a greater pressure of the spur.

Apply the spur at the trot (*petit trot*, small trot). - Finally, still following the same gradation, the rider and his aide habituate the horse to support the application of the spur at the trot-the hand opposing-without which, neither the gait nor the lightness would escape alteration.

All these applications of the spur are made, from the beginning, with the bridoon serving as the opposition to the resulting increase in action. But it is important to move to use of the curb as soon as the horse remains calm at the approach of the rowels, and it is *uniquely* this bit, *through the curb reins,* that the rider must use afterwards when there is need for one cause or another to enclose his mount between the steel of the bit and that of the spurs.

From this moment on, the horse "knows the spur." The rider can then use the spurs when necessary without their use producing disorder, and he is sure from then on to have impulsion when it serves his purpose, because he has taught the horse to always give his forces forward when the spur is applied to his side.

Moreover, while on the horse, the rider has an assured means of domination, because he has the facility to impede the horse from executing whatever would be contrary to the rider's wishes and to compel the horse to obey him.

So now, it is time for the rider to dismiss his aide and for he alone, from now on, to ride his pupil, who has become, from this preparatory training, entirely at the discretion of a rider who knows how to use his aids appropriately, especially his spurs.

PART TWO: **PREPARATION (Continued)**

GENERAL RECOMMENDATIONS

Stopping any disorder by the *effet d'ensemble* on the spur. - Once in the saddle, if the horse wants to try any defense whatsoever, the rider should immediately prevent it by an "*effet d'ensemble* on the spur"; and here is how to practice the effect.

The first condition of success is: *do not let the horse's head change position*. The rider must therefore have short reins. It is preferable and more certain, as we have already said, to use the curb reins for this effect. But it is essential not to give (the reins) so that the rider can prevent any movement toward the *extension* of the horse's head. At the same time, the calves close with force and, *immediately after their energetic grip*, the rider applies both spurs very frankly. The hand continues its opposition until this vigorous, graduated, and simultaneous pressure of the legs and the spurs *pushing* the mass onto the bit, which acts as a barrier, has produced immobility, or has re-established the regularity of the gait if the horse is moving and the rider judges it not useful to immobilize the horse. When lightness is manifested, the rider releases his fingers, then his spurs, and *finally* his legs.

The *effet d'ensemble* practiced this way, without hesitation, is the only means absolutely sure to prevent a defense. But even in the case where the occasion to use it does not present itself, it is required to devote a part of each session to review *the complete lesson of the spur* during the first days after the rider first mounts the horse without a cavesson.

Although the rider can dispense with this precaution, it remains a good thing to have an aide place himself *near* the horse's head-but without holding it if all goes well-while the rider is confirming the horse in the understanding of the spur. They can even put the cavesson back on, if-against all expectations-disorderly fretting surfaces.

If the horse backs up at the application of the spurs, the rider must *attaque* him vigorously with the spurs until he carries himself forward. This defense is little to be feared if the rider has followed the indicated progression well.

The horse must always carry himself (forward) onto the hand at the application of the spurs, all the more so at the *attaque* of the spurs. It must be the same in the *effet d'ensemble* at the halt, only then, there is no movement. But the horse's forces still come finish up on the bit, which makes the jaw yield.

If the horse kicks at the approach of the spur, the punishment is a lash of the whip close to the boot. Do not give more than one, but give a good whack *immediately* after the disobedience.

The effect of the whip. - The whip has the effect of dispersing the forces of the horse when he has concentrated them against the demands of the rider.

As well, when the horse gathers himself to resist, when he wants to kick, to rear, or to buck, if the rider wants to chastise him with the whip, he must apply a vigorous smack, a little behind the boot, but *one only*, so as not to provoke him to the exasperation that brings on a fight. Make sure that he does not see the whip so that he will be more taken by surprise by this punishment because in fact, he will fear another more painful punishment to come.

What is more, the whip is not always required in this case because the *effet d'ensemble* on the spur allows us to prevent all defenses, to stop all disorder, and to constrain the horse to continue his movement at all gaits and in any direction.

The twisting of the tail. - When the approach of the spur or of the leg provokes a twisting of the tail, the rider must be satisfied with spurs with rounded ends, or even with the naked heel, if the horse has enough action.

Proceed with extreme gradation. Follow a wise progression. No surprises; no strong action with the leg.

First gain the confidence of the horse.

The rider should apply the calves and keep them on the horse with light pressure so that their simple contact brings on twisting of the tail. Each time that the rider applies his legs, he leaves them pressed against the flanks until all movement of the tail has ceased. The lesson must finish by the horse ceasing to be preoccupied by the rider's legs. When the horse no longer twists his tail at all at the approach of the calves, the rider progresses from the calves to the naked heel, and when the heel no longer brings on the twisting of the tail, the rider progresses to spurs with rounded ends.

Finally, when the contact of the rounded ends leaves the horse cold, not producing in turn any twisting of the tail, the rider may *try* to apply rowels with the points blunted, but if the tail begins again to swish, it will go better to return to spurs with round ends.

Above all, the rider must abstain from any action that favors the twisting of the tail. Also, for example, if the piaffe brings on a twisting of the tail, the rider should not request it.

The only thing that comes from this twisting is a bad contraction of the muscles of the croup. If the croup contracts only to push the horse forward, the twisting is not produced. The rider must therefore avoid, as much as possible, opposing the hand to the leg to the point of bringing on twisting. If twisting is prevented, the horse's forces are more easily directed forward.

When the horse does not come back on himself (come "behind the bit," lean back, or even back up) at the approach of the legs or the spurs, and when in response to these actions, the hocks engage very frankly *to push*, the twisting disappears and the proper contractions of the croup produce impulsion.

The goal of the preliminary procedures of dressage. - The procedures of dressage that we are going to detail have as their goal for a start to lift the neck in a manner to lighten the forehand, to render facile the transfer of weight from the forehand to the hindquarters, and thus to arrive at equilibrium (proper balance).

The elevation of the neck can be obtained only by acting at the same time on the horse's head. The rider does not therefore occupy himself with the position that the latter part can take in the beginning. When the neck is well lifted, the lightness in the hand is completed by the relaxation of the jaw and the forehead more or less approaches the vertical. It then falls to the rider to steady the head in the *ramener* by the means that we will describe later.

Hand without leg-leg without hand. - The rider must apply from the beginning the principle of "leg without hand, hand without leg" anytime that he does not need-in order to prevent a defense or to make the horse feel the dominance of the rider-to make use of the *effet d'ensemble* on the spur.

In avoiding the simultaneous employment of the hand and leg, the horse understands more clearly what the rider wants of him and the rider is obliged to be more correct in the employment of his aids. Any errors committed by him appear immediately without attenuation.

In contrast, most of the time, when a rider uses the hand

and leg at the same time, the legs instinctively correct the mistakes of the hand, and, reciprocally, the hand corrects the errors of the leg.

CHAPTER I PREPARATORY WORK IN THE MIDDLE OF THE SCHOOL

Mounted and halted in the middle of the school, make a knot in the curb reins as well as a knot in the bridoon reins so as to have them very short.

The way to request lightness. - Lightness is requested when mounted the same way as it is in hand; the rider feels the mouth by taking a half-tension on the reins. If after continuing this action for a certain time, all the while slightly increasing the tension, the relaxation of the jaw takes too long to come, the resistances of weight are combated by the half-halts, those of force by vibrations.

It is only after resistances have been vanquished that an indication of movement can be given with the reins.

It is important to be able to distinguish these resistances and rein aids well. One must understand by resistances of force the contractions that the jaw opposes *voluntarily* to the hand of the rider. These *conscious* movements

by the horse enable him to push against the bit at any moment by pressing up (with the lower jaw) in a sort of nervous tic.

The weight impedes the equilibrium without the horse *wanting* to resist; compared to the forces that are the means by which the horse fights against the bit, instead of making it "jump" softly with his tongue.

But frequently, when the rider must give a half-halt

to obtain lightness, he must also use a vibration, and, inversely, when he uses a vibration, a half-halt is also necessary, considering that the horse often resists by weight and forces at the same time.

He should not forget that to give a half-halt or a vibration he must *tighten* his fingers. Hardly moving the hands at all, turn the left wrist, for example, so that the left rein would be accordingly tightened. It is the little finger that has the principal role, whichever hand is acting.

When giving a vibration, do not abandon the horse's mouth. The vibration is an invitation to yield, a light, very delicate invitation.

When working at the halt, should the rider meet a resistance to the effect of one rein acting alone, he may sometimes vanquish it quickly by displacing the croup with his leg on the same side (as the resistance).

He may then make the hindquarters turn methodically, slowly, around the shoulders (turn on the forehand), but continuously, until the relaxation of the jaw is manifested.

Work in place in the middle of the school. - In place, request lightness on the bridoon reins. Release the bridoon.

Request lightness on the curb reins. Release the curb. Then make the horse yield on each single rein alone of the bridoon and of the curb. Right bridoon rein. Right curb rein. Left bridoon rein. Left curb rein.

In these rein effects; hold the hand high to elevate the horse's neck as much as possible.

Afterwards, walk, but *while decomposing;* that is, by requesting lightness. Lower the hand, close the legs. When a forward step is obtained, release the legs and halt by the hand only. Request lightness again. Make another step forward, and so on.

Understand clearly that *the hand alone makes the jaw yield*, a principle that must be considered to be without exception, at least during the greatest part of training.

Then rein back. For this movement, as for any other, begin by having lightness; then *lift* the hand without action by the legs. If there is a sense that the weight is opposed to the obedience to this indication, *"forcer le mouvement"* ; that is, get to the rein-back by an energetic force, but one that is progressive, skillfully graduated, until a step to the rear is obtained. Then leave the horse in place for a moment. Request lightness again. Then "force" the rein-back again; stop, relax the jaw, and continue this way while reducing the intensity of the action of the bit until the weight of the rein suffices to obtain the rein-back.

After that, move on to the steps to the side (lateral movements) to the right and to the left.

Begin by requesting lightness. Then first, activate *the leg on the side to which one wants to go*.

This effect must always *precede* the action of the other leg.

It has the result of placing the hindquarters a little obliquely and preventing the haunches from leading the shoulders in the walk on two tracks, thus avoiding a step backwards.

As soon as the right leg, for example, has slightly displaced the croup to the left, the left leg closes a little farther back, during which the hand, preventing the impulsion from escaping out the front, is carried to the right, making the effect of the left rein predominant.

Ask only for one or two steps. Then halt. Make the horse light. Begin again. Alternate the steps to the side from right to left.

Following that, make reversed pirouettes (turns on

forehand), then ordinary pirouettes (turns on the haunches), following the same gradation, step-by-step and re-establishing lightness each time.

In the ordinary pirouettes, the rein on the side opposite the direction of movement should contain the haunches by its action and replace the outside leg as much as possible.

CHAPTER II AT THE WALK

The straight horse. - The rider moves on to the work at the walk on the track. From the first day, he must force himself always to maintain the horse *straight in the shoulders and the haunches*.

Moreover, this recommendation is applicable to all stages of dressage.

Maintain lightness, by decomposing at first, then without halting. - To re-establish or conserve lightness at the walk, the rider must not, as we have already said, act with the legs and hand at the same time. Here is how he should proceed.

He puts his hand in contact with the horse's mouth. If at this contact, the horse shows himself light by softly mobilizing his jaw, the hand gives (the reins). If, on the contrary, the hand meets resistances, *he halts*. He destroys the resistances by the means that he should already know. Then he requests movement with his legs while lowering his hands. Once movement is obtained, if the speed or the balance changes, he uses the leg or the hand according to the case, but always separately to re-establish speed and balance and to regulate the gait.

To be effective quickly, the rider should hold his legs

slightly off the flanks at the moment that the bit acts, and then give (the reins) only sufficiently as to no longer feel the mouth when he uses his leg. He can also move rapidly from the action of the hand to the effect of the leg, and often he will need to successively use one or the other at very close intervals. The essential point in this stage of training is to not oppose the hand to the leg, save in the case where it is necessary to use the *effet d'ensemble* on the spur. This is the key (*Tout est là*: everything is there).

During the walk, the rider must leave the horse free, such as he can. Alternate the flexions of the jaw in ramener (*mise en main*) on the curb, and on the bridoon.

As we have already described, it is best, in the beginning, *to decompose* (the force and the movement); that is, to halt to re-establish the correct balance when it is required. But later, the rider will be able to retrieve lightness while remaining at the walk. When he tries to vanquish

a resistance of weight while in movement, he should well understand that the half-halt, which renders the horse light when he weighs on the hand, is not at all a jerk. It consists of passing rapidly, but gradually, from minimum force to a greater force proportioned to the degree of resistance met. What is more, it must be directed *upward*, and not backward.

Give the half-halt only once at a time; then come back to a half-tension on the reins. This is the *proof* of the operation.

Start again, if necessary.

If in feeling the mouth, the rider meets a resistance to the action of the bit, and he believes it to come only from forces, a light vibration, continue, and not stronger at the end than at the beginning.

If the vibration does not bring any result, it is because, outside of the resistance of force, the weight is too much on the forehand. Then give the half-halt, and then a vibration; but it is preferable, in this case, to decompose (the force and the movement); that is, to halt so as to relax the jaw more quickly.

When the rider acts with one rein only, and a resistance manifests at the action of this rein, it is best to give a half-halt or vibration on the other rein of the same bit.

But he can also try to destroy a resistance on an isolated rein without halting by making the croup yield from the leg on the same side, which by carrying the haunches outside of the line of the shoulders will remove the point of support for the resistance.

When the rider wants to re-establish lightness without decomposing, he must not alter the gait of the horse. The force that combats the wrong contraction must never take over that force which maintains the movement.

As soon as the horse is light, give (the reins) completely while being attentive to the least faults that the horse may commit.

Descent of the hand. - From time to time, halt; adjust the curb reins; with the horse light and his head well placed, open the left hand, and lower the right hand, which takes the end of the knotted reins, down to the horse's neck.

As soon as the horse moves his head, take the reins back. This is the descent of the hand.

In the same fashion, try descents of the hand while at the walk. But when the horse is light, champs his bit, and the rider has given to him completely, *do not permit the displacement of the head, nor the lowering of the neck.*

Take back the horse as soon as he abandons his balance; that is, as soon as he lowers his head or increases his pace.

Try using this principle, to let him go freely.

But he must have this freedom only in balance with lightness, so that he learns early to carry himself correctly with his head well placed.

Only when the horse's education is advanced can the rider come to the complete descent of the hand or of the hand and leg.

From walk to rein-back. - Pass frequently from walk to rein-back. As soon as the lightness is correct, depart at the walk. Rein-back, walk, etc.

Turns on small circles on the pressure of the outside rein. - The rider then begins the turns on small circles on the outside rein, (counter rein (The modern fourth rein effect-*rêne contraire d'opposition en avant du garrot* or *rêne des épaules*, counter rein of opposition in front of the withers or shoulder rein, (Licart, p. 14,))).

Here is how to proceed.

With the knotted reins (the curb or the bridoon alternatively) held in only one hand, the rider carries that hand toward the side to which the horse will turn so that the outside rein acts alone.

If, at the rider's action, the jaw remains flexible with the horse's nose turned slightly toward the outside of the circle, the weight of the neck shifts to the inside. Then if the shoulders incline frankly and softly to the centre of the circle, the rider gives (the reins) immediately.

If, on the contrary, the pressure of the outside reins meets a resistance, he makes it disappear by the usual means and the inside rein acts discretely at the same time to aid the turn.

The essential point is not a marked bend in the neck. It is the mobility of the jaw; in a word, perfect lightness.

Meanwhile, the weight of the forehand must be carried toward the inside of the circle so as to shift more weight to the inside shoulder and leave a greater liberty of action to the outside shoulder, which has to follow a longer track. But as the training advances, the end of the horse's nose should turn less and less to the outside. The rider can even come to obtain the change of direction on the exterior rein with a slight bend of the neck to the inside.

In the beginning the rider can request the turns with the horse's head high and more or less horizontal, but as the education of the horse advances, the rider must execute them with the horse in ramener.

So the rider prepares for the turns by working at the halt, requesting the inclination of the weight of the neck to the right or to the left by the pressure of the opposite rein.

This pressure is produced by lifting the hand and carrying it slightly backwards (by rotating the wrist to bring the little finger up and back) in the direction of the diagonal hind leg corresponding to the acting rein (left rein to right hind (left diagonal) shifts weight to right shoulder).

Turns on the inside rein. - Intersperse these turns on small circles on the outside rein with turns on the inside rein, which must also provoke the relaxation of the jaw, at the same time as it indicates the direction (modern first rein effect, *rêne d'ouverture (rêne du bout du nez)*, opening rein (rein of the end of the nose), Licart, p. 13). Continue soft action on this rein until the end of the exercise.

Serpentine. - Afterwards, the rider executes the serpentine.

So that it will be well done, he must turn sharply on arriving at the track and then go perfectly straight and perpendicularly to the other wall.

The serpentine is executed either on the outside rein or on the inside rein (direct rein (modern third rein effect, *rêne directe d'opposition (rêne des hanches)*, direct rein of opposition (haunches rein)), Licart, p. 13.), but it is much better to work this movement on the outside rein (counter rein (see *rêne contraire d'opposition en avant du garrot*, above)).

Changes of hand on two tracks. - In order to be able to execute the change of hand on two tracks, the rider begins by requesting only one or two steps to the side as he arrives at the opposite wall; later he asks for three or four.

Then he *tient les hanches* (holds the haunches, half-passes) from the centre line, and finally from one wall to the other.

In the steps to the side (lateral movements, note that the Baucherists practiced shoulder-in only rarely, or not at all), both legs can, and even must, be used at the same time. These two actions do not contradict each other, in that one pushes to the side and the other forward; one must be a little behind the other.

Lateral movements (steps to the side), the head, followed by the croup to the wall. - On the track, request the movement head to the wall (haunches in, travers). As soon as the jaw stiffens, halt in the oblique position; relax the jaw, and depart again. Use the least hand and leg possible.

Proceed the same way for croup to the wall (haunches out, renvers). Go slowly. Relax the jaw often.

Alternate these movements.

In the lateral movements, the opposing rein (the support rein (modern second rein effect, *rêne d'appui (rêne de l'encolure)*, pressure or support rein (neck rein), Licart, p. 13.)) should replace, as much as possible, the leg on the same side.

As soon as the movement takes shape, move from the use of the leg to that of the hands as much as possible.

After the head to the wall or the croup to the wall, the rider should always straighten the horse before asking for the opposite exercise. Then he can put the horse back in balance, make him light, and have only one force to conquer in order to execute the inverse movement.

In the work on two tracks, if the rider meets resistance at the pressure of one rein, instead of taking an action a little strong and fixed, that which is practiced ordinarily, he should replace this action with a half-halt, a second, a third, etc., if it is necessary.

When passing from the croup to the wall to the head to the wall, or the inverse, and when straightening the horse, prevent the forehand from advancing before the new position is given. (When staying on the same track, slow the shoulders while moving the croup from right to left or the inverse.

Otherwise, having reversed direction through a half volte maintaining the haunches-in position and wanting to change to the croup to the wall (haunches-out) upon arriving back at the track, the rider, traveling in half-pass back to the track, half-halts to slow the shoulders at the track to allow the haunches to pass the shoulders laterally to create, with the influence of the outside leg, the new position for the croup to the wall. Similarly, but not identically, when having reversed direction through a half volte in the haunches-out position to change from the croup to the wall to the head to the wall, the rider, traveling again in half-pass toward the track, but in the opposite bend with the head to the wall, maintains the bend with an active outside leg and half-halts to slow the shoulders while changing direction from the diagonal to the track.)

In the head to the wall movement (haunches-in, travers), when the rider passes through a corner, from left to right for example (a right turn), the right leg should slow down the croup slightly to leave time for the shoulders to make their larger arc of the circle as they accelerate their step a little.

In the head and croup to the wall, the rider's leg should indicate only the action and his hand only the position.

Moreover, the same as the hand must not act in a continuous fashion, the legs must only stay on the flanks such as it is necessary; simply stated, their effect must be not fixed, but intermittent.

Small counter-changes of hand on two tracks. - From the track, half-pass (*appuyer*) two steps to the inside; walk two steps straight; half-pass two steps to the outside to return to the track and so on.

Repeat this work crossing the school length-wise (down the center line).

Pirouettes, ordinary and reversed. - Pirouettes, ordinary and reversed, are begun by decomposing them.

Request a step of pirouette. Halt. Make the horse light. Request another step, halt, and so on.

Then execute them two steps by two steps. Then by quarter-pirouette, and finally by half-pirouette.

Do not use the hand and the leg at the same time.

Try to make the ordinary pirouettes by the hand only.

In the reversed pirouettes, try to make the leg act alone, without the aid of the reins. If the horse weighs on the hand, half-halt without the leg on the required rein, but principally on the inside rein. Continue the movement in the same way.

If the horse leans or steps back, inside leg, without the hand of course.

When the horse executes the ordinary pirouette well, and the rider requests this movement, as soon as the pirouette, indicated by the hand, has begun, he must release the reins. The horse should finish on his own.

Now to execute the ordinary pirouette at the walk, since the croup should be fixed in place, stop the hindquarters with a half-halt, principally on the outside rein. Immediately afterwards the hand is carried toward the inside to give direction to the forehand which has to rotate about the hindquarters.

As soon as the direction is given, descent of the hand. The movement should finish on its own.

Be on guard against any backward tendency in the ordinary pirouettes.

Voltes and half voltes, ordinary and reversed, on two tracks. - For these two movements, proceed as for the pirouettes, by decomposing them. Do not ask for the volte until having obtained the half volte, and do not try the half volte without taking the time to execute it step by step, and then two steps by two steps, halting to re-establish lightness after each new request.

In the work on half voltes, ordinary and reversed, the important point is that the horse *does not advance* at the end of the movement. The horse must arrive parallel to the track, and halt there without having gained any ground. This indicates that the weight is in balance and not too much on the shoulder.

Prolonged rein-back on the track. - Intersperse often all the work at the walk with requests for the rein-back. When the rein-back is regular, and can be obtained easily, prolong the movement on the track, alternating the effect of the curb and the bridoon, without letting the horse stop or modify his cadence.

Foule (crowd). - This exercise consists of turning very tightly, and in all directions, in the middle of the school avoiding the track, without stopping.

When several riders (thus the "crowd") execute this exercise, each one must try not to go in the same direction as his neighbor.

The hand acts alone by the pressure of the outside rein. As soon as the jaw is flexible, give (the reins). If the resistance is prolonged, conquer it *en marchant* (on the march, in motion, without halting) by the known procedures.

As needed, decompose (the force and the movement) by halting to relax the jaw.

The rider tries the descent of the hand each time that direction is given and that the lightness is good.

Afterward, leaving the reins on the neck as often as possible, try to ride the *foule* on the leg only.

The hand comes when it is necessary, but then the legs release. It is the inside leg that should produce the turn.

Afterwards, the *foule* can be ridden using all the airs of the school (*manège*) on two tracks, one after the other in no particular order.

If several riders are working on this exercise at the same time, they must pay attention that two neighboring horses are never making the same figure.

Finally the rider executes the *foule* replacing the turns by ordinary pirouettes or by interspersing the two. He must take care that the horse does not slow his pace too much at the moment of the stop for the pirouette. He starts it when the hind legs are fixed.

Getting to the ramener. - The important point-at the halt above all, but equally at the walk-is to obtain, from the beginning, lightness from the horse with the head elevated. The ramener comes later by way of the flexibility of the jaw. But *the jaw must always yield first* while the neck is very high and without the head making any movement.

Stay with these exercises for a very long time. Do not move beyond them until they are executed perfectly.

"Go very slowly to bring the training along rapidly."

This recommendation to demand lightness from the beginning, while the neck is very elevated and steady, applies to the curb as well as the bridoon. Relax the jaw with the head high, and often nearly horizontal. It is only then that the head may be permitted to approach the perpendicular. But with a horse prepared this way, the ramener is produced quickly, and soon becomes easy to maintain.

The rider may take the trot only after all the work at the walk has been done with regularity, lightness, the neck self-supported, and the head well placed.

CHAPTER III AT THE COLLECTED TROT (*petit trot*: **small trot**)

Repeat at the collected trot, all the work executed at the walk. - Once the horse is consistently light at the walk, put him into the collected trot using the leg with the hand lowered. (Faverot did not distinguish among working, collected, medium, and extended trot, but as for the distinction *petit trot*, small trot, collected trot, and *grand trot*, large trot, lengthened trot; the *petit trot* was used for dressage in the school, and *grand trot* was used largely outdoors. Faverot did not use the *trot enlevé*, rising trot.)Then feel the mouth. If the lightness has disappeared, halt, relax the jaw, then depart at the walk again, and then the collected trot.

It is necessary in the beginning for the rider to decompose the movements without end, above all with those horses whose gaits are unbalanced.

As soon as he feels the balance compromised, as soon as the cadence loses its regularity, halt, relax the jaw, make him light. Then, request the movement again. Pay the greatest attention to departs at the walk and at the trot. Make sure that the gait is, from the very beginning, very correct, very regular.

At the trot, as at the walk, leave the horse free as much as possible as soon as he is light, that is, in balance; and is doing well at what is being asked of him.

"When he believes that he is his own master, that is when he is our slave."

Repeat at the trot all the work executed at the walk. The same recommendations for circles and for all the other exercises.

When the rider requests a new movement of whatever kind on two tracks, he must start at the walk, then take the trot for a stride or two in the oblique position, then take the walk again while staying on two tracks, and so on, always increasing the number of strides at the trot.

Make these demands with a very gradual progression.

Depart at the collected trot from the halt. Halt from the trot. - Next, depart at the collected trot from the halt. Halt; depart again at the collected trot.

Try the descent of the hand often, even in the lateral movements.

After every lateral movement, never forget to straighten the horse before requesting the inverse movement.

In the work at the trot, when the rider tries to re-establish balance without halting, above all he must avoid jerks. Feel the mouth well, before giving a half-halt for example. Any brusque action renders the horse uncertain in his gaits.

At the end of the half voltes, ordinary or reversed, at the trot, in finishing with the half-pass (*en tenant les hanches*), as he did at the walk, the rider pays great attention that the horse does not advance (the rider half-halts to slow the shoulders, and increases the action of the outside leg to bring the haunches in line with the shoulders, straightening the horse, before he proceeds straight on the track).

Also, if in the lateral movements, there is a resistance to the pressure of the rein, replace the fixed action on that rein with one or several successive half-halts if that is necessary.

Often use both legs at the same time in the lateral movements.

Recall that the inside leg, on the side to which the horse moves, above all pushes forward, and serves also to avoid the horse backing up or the haunches leading.

When the *foule* is well done, try to make the turns in this exercise on the inside leg, the reins resting on the neck, or at least not acting, as long as the gait does not become rushed.

Try more than ever to keep the horse always very straight.

Pass from the collected trot to the rein-back. - Intersperse the rein-back into all the work requested while the horse is at the collected trot.

To do this, the gait must be well cadenced and the horse light, then halt by an effect of the hand that is rapid, energetic, but soft and adroitly graduated, in a fashion so as to produce the rein-back, as soon as the forward movement is checked, and without an appreciable time at the halt.

Foule **to the rear**. - Then when the rein-back can continue of itself during the descent of the hand, try to make the *foule* to the rear, that is: execute turns in reverse on each leg individually, without the aid of the hand, in every direction.

For the work to be completely regular, the reins must rest on the neck. The changes of direction must be produced by the leg on the inside of the turn.

It is well understood, of course, that at the beginning of each turn, the hand comes anytime it is necessary to help the horse to understand what is demanded of him. While the hand acts, release the legs.

How the neck must be lifted. - In all this first part of dressage the rider must look to lift the neck as much as possible. He is acting on the weight when he demands this elevation; but it is important that in transferring the weight to the hindquarters, *the forces that produce the forward movement not be at all diminished*. It is necessary on the other hand that, in requesting the action that produces the force that pushes, this same force *carry in the direction of the movement only the small quantity of weight necessary to the movement,* and that the balance be not altered, that the transfer of weight remain equally easy in any direction, *after the movement is obtained, just as before.*

When a horse has a strong tendency to lower his neck, the rider must hold his hands very high, above the ears if necessary, until the jaw yields softly in this position. He gives (the reins) then, but takes again, as soon as the head lowers, constantly having the hands very elevated to prevent the horse from burying himself.

It is necessary with such a horse to stay at the work at the halt and collected gaits for a very long time, and not to take the curb reins until the rider has obtained a constant and easy elevation on the bridoon.

Once the weight is in balance, once the neck is elevated and self-supporting, the rider may destroy the resistances of force when needed; and then the head with a flexible poll, left to itself, comes to its most comfortable position.

Next we come to the ramener. - Then it is the hand, always acting *alone*; that is, without it being opposed to a simultaneous action of the leg, and of course without taking from the movement, without altering the speed of the gait, that gradually obtains the ramener. Beginning with the effect of each rein *isolated* at first, then crisscrossed (bridoon rein from one side, curb rein from the opposite side), then finishing by the simultaneous use of both bridoon reins or both curb reins. All the work at the collected trot is repeated successively this way with stronger and more sustained requests on the part of the rider.

When the rider looks to bring the head to the perpendicular by using each rein in its turn *isolated*, often he can also obtain prompt results by the following procedures:

As soon as the rein, held a little short, meets a resistance, he can make this resistance yield, without modifying the gait, by slightly displacing the croup on the pressure of the leg on the same side.

He continues said lateral effect (right rein and right leg, or left rein and left leg) which throws the hindquarters a little outside the line of the shoulders, just until the relaxation of the jaw is produced, soon followed by the approach of the head to the perpendicular.

It is to be remarked that the action of one rein and that of the leg on the same side aid each other mutually instead of opposing reciprocally, such as that produced in a diagonal effect.

Diagonal effects. - It is for this reason that diagonal effects, besides being inapplicable to rapid gaits, should be avoided. They are composed of two opposite forces in which one pushes in one direction and the other holds in the direction diametrically opposed. These forces annul each other, or more or less work against each other, if they are not equal. They often result in provoking the horse to resist their double constraint, leading the horse to contract certain of his muscles incorrectly. What is more, the diagonal effect stops, more or less, the play of the shoulder on the side of the rein that serves to produce it, and bends the horse which then more and more makes a habit of making himself crooked at the various gaits.

CHAPTER IV THE *RASSEMBLER*

Before starting the *rassembler* mounted, the ramener must be complete; that is, the horse must conserve his lightness well at the walk with his forehead perpendicular, at first on the action of the legs closed energetically, then on a progressive pressure of the spurs pushed to a strong pressure, the hand opposing of course. It is necessary also that "the movement of the forces forward," which makes the horse depart from the walk to the trot, be easy on the spur, the lightness remaining unchanged.

When the training has come to this point, the rider can undertake the *rassembler* because, if the effects used to produce it more or less ruin the ramener, it is still easy to re-establish it with or even without the spur.

How to request the *rassembler*. - To request the *rassembler*, first put the horse on the track. At the halt, place him very straight and make him light; then the alternating vibration of both legs, while softly holding with the hand. As soon as there is a little bit of mobility in the horse's legs, give (the reins), caress him, and let him rest. Demand very little at the beginning.

In working to these principles, the rider has difficulty making the horse understand what the rider is asking for, he can use the whip as an aid from time to time, which then acts, as it does in hand, on one of the flanks or on top of the croup.

Ask for lightness again at each halt. Restart often on each hand. Take care to walk one or two steps after each round of *rassembler*.

During all this work, do not neglect to straighten the horse *as soon as he becomes crooked*, and to seek mobility of the legs only once the horse is very straight and light. Always advance a little in the *rassembler* in order to avoid the horse coming "behind the bit" or backing.

If the horse "crow hops," he does so in defense; reprimand him immediately with half-halts given with tact. As soon as there is calm and light mobility, give (the reins) completely, and caress him. But never request the *rassembler* before the lightness is perfect.

Such as the horse remains light, any defense is impossible to him. In effect, for him to defend himself, he must stiffen part of his body, and the stiffness of that part of his body would be translated to stiffness in his jaw. As soon as the rider can force the horse to keep the lightness in his mouth, then he can prevent *resistance*, or defense.

When, after the *rassembler*, the rider halts by an *effet d'ensemble*, it is preferable that the horse's legs do not remain engaged under the mass (of his body). The *effet d'ensemble* must re-establish the ramener, and give back to the horse his normal alignment.

PART THREE: PUTTING IT TOGETHER

CHAPTER I DEPARTS AND WORK AT THE CANTER

When the *rassembler* in hand has become very easy, when the ramener has become well fixed at the walk and at the collected trot, and finally, when the rider has obtained the beginning of the *rassembler*, it is time to try the canter departs.

There are many ways to make a horse depart at the canter from the walk.

The principal methods to request the canter. - When the rider has a horse that is not at all familiar with this gait, it is not correct to look for the *rassembler* right away.

Push him on to the hand as if the rider wants to take up the trot. Then the hands are carried to the left for a depart to the right for example, the left rein held shorter than the right, and the two legs close with nearly equal force, the left a little behind the girth.

The canter having been produced, as soon as there is an appearance of lightness, reward.

After a dozen strides, come back to the walk.

Start over many times on each hand.

At the moment the rider gives the position for the canter, if he *feels* the muscle contractions that would produce a false depart, he should prevent the movement, take up the walk again, and begin again to place the horse in position.

He should try to feel when the horse is *going* to take a defective position.

If he acts after this defective position is already taken, that is bad. It is even worse if he does not halt the horse before the first bound of the depart.

If the rider notices while using the bridoon that "the forces have gotten too far away" (*les forces s'eloignent trop*), that the head is too far in front and that the hocks are not engaged enough, that they are too far from the centre (of the horse), take the curb alone, but afterwards, come back to the bridoon from time to time.

As soon as the departs are easily requested this way, use the following method to put the horse to the canter.

With the horse on the track at the walk and light, begin by applying the legs with the inside leg dominant. Then *as soon as* the action is thus augmented by the leg, carry the hand to the outside to give the position that engenders the movement. Take great care with these departs.

For the canter to the right for example, first look for lightness on the right rein; then, the impulsion being sufficient, lift the hand to the left while approaching the body (with the little finger by a rotation of the wrist).

The action should be given almost exclusively with the inside leg, so as to keep the horse straight by preventing the croup from coming from the side opposite to that from where the hand is carried.

Once the canter is produced, at each descent of the

forehand, half-halt to cadence the gait, which from the depart must be as regular as the pendulum of a clock.

When the rider can keep the canter, change the reins often, one hand only holding the bridoon, then the curb, then the bridoon. During these changes of the reins, the gait should not vary.

If the speed increases, decompose (the force and the movement). Stop short, relax the jaw, and then depart again (in balance).

Departs at the counter-canter. - After that, ask for the counter-canter.

To do this, at the walk carry the shoulders of the horse to the inside in a manner to make him take the degree of obliquity of a quarter of a "croup to the wall," and depart at the canter in this position by the same means as above, but using, from the beginning, the opposite aids (right rein and leg for the depart on the left lead while on the right hand).

Make four strides of canter that way and come back to the walk; re-establish lightness, depart again, etc.

But get to the point, as soon as possible, of obtaining the departs at the counter-canter with the rein and leg on the wall side acting as the principal aids.

Afterwards, alternate counter-canter departs with true canter departs.

In all the canter work, try more than ever to keep the horse absolutely straight and light.

Method to re-straighten the horse. - In the beginning, as soon as the horse becomes more or less crooked, as soon as resistance is manifested, decompose (the force and the movement), that is halt, re-straighten, make him light, and depart again.

Later when the rider is ready to try to combat the resistances without halting, he should re-straighten his horse by the following procedure: if the horse advances his croup to the right, in the canter to the right for example, the rider should, when the horse's jaw is flexible and soft, lightly apply the left rein to the neck in a manner to shift the weight of the forehand onto the right shoulder, which has the consequence, more or less, of making the haunches move to the left, and of bringing the nose to the same side.

In a word, the rider corrects the bend by giving the horse, by a delicate effect of the hand, the inverse bend. But in doing this, he must avoid using his leg.

To re-establish lightness while at the canter, do not alter the horse's pace in any way while combating his resistances.

In acting against the resistance of weight, always look to lift the neck as much as possible, but without taking anything from the force necessary to the movement.

Relax the jaw and let the head gradually approach the perpendicular.

Descent of the hand. - As soon as the rider has good lightness at the canter, he can try the descents of the hand and repeat them often.

Furthermore, try to use the least hand and the least leg possible in all the work at this gait.

Rein-back. - Pass frequently from the canter to the rein-back by the effect of the elevation of the hands without leg, an effect that more than ever must be skillfully graduated while being a little energetic.

Depart again at the canter immediately after the halt from the rein-back.

Small Circles. - With the horse very light, describe circles of small diameter, asking for them by the pressure of the outside rein against the neck to transfer the weight to the inside shoulder, which brings, according to the principle, the nose slightly to the outside and *"fait tomber"* ("makes to fall") the forehand towards the centre of the circle.

Canter on two tracks. - Now move to the canter on two tracks.

Begin by the head and the croup to the wall.

For this movement, first take the shortened reins in one hand (curb or bridoon).

With the horse moving obliquely (on the track) at the walk, ask for only a few strides of canter on two tracks and return to the walk.

Each time that the forehand goes down in the canter *sur les hanches* (on the haunches, very collected canter), make an accentuated upward half-halt, without advancing the hand, *to lift* the horse and cadence the gait. The hand must lift each time that the forelegs touch the ground (Faverot may well have not seen photographs of the horse at the canter), and then lower more rapidly than it was lifted. The movement of the hand must be very rhythmic.

The rider should act more with the outside rein and outside leg so as to push the horse with two forces on the same side. The movements of the hand should be scarcely apparent.

If the horse advances in the croup to the wall (loses his oblique angle by moving his shoulders toward the track pushing onto his forehand trailing his haunches behind), it is because there is too much weight on the forehand;

lift him at each descent of the forehand by an energetic half-halt.

Remaining in croup to the wall and without straightening, collect the canter in renvers to the right and to the left (shallow serpentine maintaining the croup to the wall position).

In all of these movements on two tracks at the canter, halt often, relax the jaw, then depart again, etc.

To obtain and then to maintain the canter, the hand and the leg should not at all act at the same time. The hand places (the horse in position), ceases its effect; the legs give the action and then release; then the hand lifts the forehand, even with substantial force if it is necessary, understanding that this action shifts to the hindquarters the weight that has surcharged the forehand.

Then the hand lowers again. Then the legs come if the action is dying, etc. If the leg and the hand act simultaneously, their effects tend to annul each other and produce contractions.

Change of hand on the diagonal. - To get to the change of hand on the diagonal at the canter on two tracks, begin the movement at the walk; then, make two or three strides of canter on two tracks; go back to the walk, still on two tracks; depart again at the canter, return to the walk, etc.

After increasing the number of strides at the canter, finally try the change of hand on the diagonal at the canter without passing through the walk

In this movement on two tracks, try as much as possible to make one or two steps with the descent of the hand.

Do not forget that in the canter on two tracks, as in any lateral movement at the other gaits, both legs can and

should be used at the same time; one pushes forward and the other to the side. The latter is placed a little more to the rear than the other.

But when the training has advanced, the hand should do almost all of it; especially the outside rein.

Pay close attention to distinguish what causes mistakes, whether it is the action or the position.

More and more, reduce the force of the aids employed.

If there is a resistance to the pressure of a rein, do not insist on a *fixed* action. Replace it immediately with a half-halt, followed by a second, by a third, etc.

Afterward, cross the school at the canter on two tracks on a line perpendicular to the long sides, maintaining the horse parallel to these same long sides and without advancing from the line (full pass).

As needed, decompose this movement by halting to re-establish lightness.

Half voltes on two tracks at the canter. - Then begin an ordinary half volte on two tracks (haunches-in) at the walk. Finish it by several strides at the canter.

The same gradation is used for a half volte reversed.

Finish by executing these half voltes entirely at the canter.

Pirouettes at the canter. - To prepare for the pirouettes at the canter, execute smaller half voltes on two tracks, starting at the walk and finishing at the canter.

Repeat them often, at the same place, returning to the point of the depart by the inverse movement.

In this work, be careful that the horse does not advance; but at the same time, avoid the horse beginning to feel sucked back due to overloading his haunches.

Finally, move to the ordinary pirouette.

Begin as before at the walk and finish by one or two bounds of the canter.

Thus the rider comes to make a complete half-pirouette entirely at the canter. In this movement, the horse must be very straight. As soon as the rider can execute the half-pirouette entirely at the canter, the least use of the legs possible. If he uses them too much, they will bring disorder, stamping, losing the bound of the canter.

Volte on two tracks at the canter. - For the volte, start one on two tracks (haunches-in) at the walk in the middle of the school. Then, make a stride of canter and return to the walk; then, make two strides of canter, and so on until the entire volte is made at the canter in haunches-in.

In the work at the canter on two tracks, there may come a moment when the rein on the side to which one is going (ordinarily the inside rein) is too powerful and leaves the croup behind (the forehand "advances"). Then use it with the least possible contact and use the outside rein with pressure on the neck. However this pressure must be delicate. The horse is thereby *pushed* to the side that the rider wants to travel. Moreover, this action makes a light opposition to the croup, which, without this effect, would be left a little behind.

Depart at the canter by the hand, without the leg. - The training should reach the point where the rider can put his horse to the canter by the effect of the hand *without the use of the leg*.

To accomplish this effect, while at the walk on the right hand, for example, carry the hand, which is holding knotted reins (either curb or bridoon), to the left and a little to the rear (by rotation of the wrist bringing the little finger backward), and give a half-halt. If the horse slows, give (the reins); push him forward with the leg, and then begin the same effect on the reins again; two, three, four little half-halts, if necessary, until the bound of the canter is produced.

But if the pace of the walk slows, stop all action of the hand, and push him forward. Give the half-halts a little more strongly to sufficiently lighten the forehand if there is a lot of weight to shift.

As soon as the depart is obtained, the hand should release, holding itself ready to retake the reins if needed. This is the sole means of seeing what effect has been produced. It will show what degree of equilibrium has been achieved and whether there is too much weight on the forehand, etc.

It is necessary to have plenty of finesse in the actions of the hand.

This work, very delicate, is extremely important. The rider learns to act on the weight without taking back from the force that pushes. To the degree that the half-halts combat only the weight, they do not diminish the impulsion, but, as soon as they act on the force, they slow or even stop the horse.

Continue departs requested this way until the horse understands them and gives them easily; do not press; above all, be calm and have perseverance.

The first depart often takes a long time to appear. When the rider has been successful, repeat the departs until the horse does them easily on both hands. Then execute this work in the middle of the school. Never use the leg when the hand acts; but as soon as there is a slowing, push firmly; use the spur as needed.

The rider should come eventually to the canter depart from the rein-back on the same effect of the hand employed for the canter depart from the walk.

This work gives excellent results when it is practiced as follows:

At the halt, with the horse's back turned to a long side of the school, rein back to the wall.

Then depart at the canter and continue to the opposite track. Rein back anew. Depart again at the canter, and repeat the exercise.

Canter on two tracks, without the leg. - Then the rider repeats all the work of the canter *sur les hanches* (on the haunches, very collected), trying to execute them without using the leg.

For good execution of the movements on two tracks at this gait (the canter), it is necessary, according to principle, to make the rider's leg on the side toward which he wants to travel obliquely *act first*. This is to avoid the haunches leading and to maintain or give impulsion. But when the horse keeps his balance easily, if there is a sufficient degree of action, the rider should quiet this leg. In the same way, the rider should *quiet the other leg as soon as it has indicated the direction of travel* in the *pas de coté* (steps to the side, lateral movements); the head to the wall, the croup to the wall, etc.

So, with the horse at the walk on two tracks, request a depart at the collected canter on two tracks with half-halts and without the aid of the leg. At the beginning, be content with a stride or two. It is understood that when the action diminishes or ceases, the hand gives (the reins) completely, ceasing its action, and the legs reactivate the impulsion.

Then the hand begins again to request the canter depart. To obtain this canter depart, the half-halts can be given on one or the other rein, as the case may be, or for sure, on both at once.

Also, if the weight is on the forehand, or the forehand appears heavy, the rein on the side of the direction of travel should be the principal actor, or even act alone.

If the hindquarters are trailing the forehand, it is the other rein that should give the half-halts to chase the haunches by an opposition. It is a question of tact.

Be careful that the effect of the hand is a half-halt and not a jerk. Also ask for canter departs on two tracks in the change of hand on the diagonal, in the head or croup to the wall, etc.

Act with the hand only when the action is well sustained at the walk. When it ceases, stop the hand, then use the leg.

In the same way, once the canter on two tracks is obtained, if the action does not continue, stop any effect of the hand and use the leg.

Be content, as usual, with two or three strides of the canter on two tracks without leg.

Halt often; relax the jaw.

Frequently give the horse several minutes of rest with absolute immobility in perfect balance.

In the same order of ideas, ask for voltes and half voltes on two tracks while using the leg as little as one can.

Prepare for the ordinary pirouettes at the canter without use of the leg by using half voltes, tightened without exaggeration and executed on the hand alone.

Guard against haunches leading with horses that too easily come back on themselves. If so, the hand then must redouble its delicacy.

To execute the ordinary half pirouette the rider must, in the beginning, alternate the effects of the hand and the action of the leg. By avoiding using both of them together, the rider will soon be able to do without the leg completely.

Canter depart on the leg only. - In order to perfect the balance of the horse, it is a good thing, not only to exercise him at the canter depart on the hand only, but also, inversely, to try to obtain the depart at this gait using only the leg.

To do this, with the reins on the neck, or held at their extremity so that they have no action on the mouth, apply the left leg, for example, at the walk to the flank of the horse and activate the right leg with successive little taps a bit more forward until the (right lead) canter depart is produced.

If at the moment of contact with the legs, the horse takes up the trot, release the legs entirely, and by one or more half-halts, prevent the weight from transferring to the forehand. Once the walk is re-established, begin again to request the canter depart on the leg only to the right.

When this result is obtained, alternate the canter depart on the hand with the canter depart on the leg.

Execute the same work on the left lead.

Afterward, depart at the trot from the walk on equal and progressive pressure from both legs.

But understand that the difference between the means employed to obtain the canter or the trot on the leg is more an exercise in equestrian tact than an application of theory.

Canter depart by the rein and leg on the side opposite the requested lead, without making the horse crooked. - It remains for us to say how the rider can produce a canter depart on the lateral aids, the rein and leg on the side opposite the lead desired, while the horse remains very straight in shoulders and haunches.

This method of obtaining the canter (or the gallop) above all finds its application in outdoor equitation. It presents an advantage in that it allows the rider to always use it to put his horse to the canter from the beginning to the end of training.

Prepare this work as follows.

With the horse very light, put him on a circle of small diameter to the right by means of the pressure of the left rein (curb or bridoon) on the neck. Then, obtain the canter to the right, passing through the collected trot if necessary, using the left rein and left leg as the principal agents.

The left rein must be the predominate aid, and in a way push the forehand to the right, the nose of the horse remaining a little to the left. The rider's left leg, while communicating the necessary action, must avoid "traversing" the horse (pushing the croup too far to the right) so that the shoulders and haunches will remain exactly on the circle described.

When this preparatory work is acceptable on each hand, it is time to move to canter departs on a straight line, with the horse remaining very straight and the rider is still using the rein and leg opposite the required lead.

Then, the rider must give the horse the position by shifting his weight, at first very slightly, to the hindquarters, and then by pushing him, so to say, toward the right and forward.

To do this, with the horse light and in ramener, request the canter on the right lead, for example. Depart from the walk or the collected trot, lift the hand, bring it closer (by rotating the wrist, little finger backward) to the body, the left rein acting almost alone in this half-halt in a progressive intensity skillfully graduated. End the effect by carrying the hand to the right in a manner to produce on the neck with this same left rein, a light *pulsation* toward the right. At the moment when the hand *begins* this effect, the left leg must act by a pressure in proportion to the required increase in impulsion, if the horse does not have the degree of action sufficient to jump into the canter.

The pressure of the left rein on the neck tends to produce a certain *pli* (slight bend) to the left that makes the end of the nose and the croup move slightly *to the left* while the shoulders are pushed to the right. A delicate pressure of the left leg would then not make the horse crooked.

If necessary, the right rein should prevent the nose from turning to the left and, like the right leg, should be ready to intervene in the case of need.

Repeat these half-halts until the canter has been obtained, and ask, of course, for the departs on each lead.

Keep at this work for a long time, interspersed with frequent halts followed by the rein-back. Also, with the horse very light, depart at the canter to the rear on the same effects.

Come to the point, as previously, of doing without the leg as much as possible, if not entirely, for these departs.

It is to be remarked that this manner of requesting the gallop is very analogous to the action of "*rouler*" (to roll), which a rider often uses at the end of a race to allow the horse to use all of his resources, repeating it at each stride of the forelegs.

CHAPTER II THE LENGTHENED TROT (*GRAND TROT*)

Work at the lengthened trot. - When the work at the canter begins to be well executed, and the horse easily holds the collected and round position that comes with the gait, it is time to exercise him in lengthening all his *ressorts* (springs, joints, resources) from time to time while keeping him light and in ramener.

To do this, the rider first takes up the collected trot, and when the gait is very regular, progressively lengthens it.

There may come a time when the horse, having a great disposition to engage his hocks, to collect himself, becomes difficult to maintain in the trot, even a slow trot after exercises at the canter. In this case, the rider should cease entirely requesting the latter gait for a while until the trot comes easily.

Moreover, when a position becomes very familiar to a horse, it is always at the cost of the facility with which he takes up another. In that case, the rider must only request of the horse those positions that he is at pain to conserve until the situation improves.

If the lengthened trot is not well formed, or if lightness is lost, stop short, relax (the jaw), and depart again. Remember, twenty times if necessary, the rider must decompose (the force and the movement) until the horse frankly starts the requested gait.

This principle, moreover, is as applicable to the canter as to the lengthened trot. Each stride must be strictly similar to its neighbor in speed and cadence.

Above all take care with the first step of the depart.

In the beginning, do not try to re-establish balance while in motion: instead, halt, and relax (the jaw). When calm and lightness have returned, but not before, request the lengthened trot again.

Descents of the hand. - When the gait is very frank and well settled and lightness persists, lower the hand as it holds the reins, knotted as always, at their extremity, and let them act no more as long as the horse conserves his balance. The rider should then progressively lower the reins entirely, but hold them ready for any eventuality. The rider takes them back adroitly and nimbly as soon as there is cause to use them again.

When the horse goes freely and without bother, the head high and well placed, the neck supported by itself, try to leave the reins on the neck as long as the equilibrium remains intact. But take back the horse as soon as his balance is lost, *as soon as he lowers his neck* or increases his pace.

Outside at the lengthened trot, it is not necessary that the horse champ his bit when he delivers himself well. It suffices that he does not pull, that he has his neck high, the head remaining softly *fixed* at a position close to the perpendicular, and that he goes energetically and very straight forward, but ready to play his bit if the rider comes to use the reins for whatever reason.

CHAPTER III CHANGES OF LEAD AT THE CANTER

Method to begin lead changes. - To teach the horse to change lead at the canter at the wish of the rider, execute a diagonal change of hand at this gait in the half-pass in a fashion to finish at four strides or less from the corner to have time to act before the horse bends himself to turn.

Arriving at the opposite track, push with the legs, making the outside predominant. Receive the weight right away on the hand, which is then carried toward the wall principally with an active outside rein.

The rider should, therefore, from the start, use as the principal aids the rein and leg opposite the requested lead to vanquish those resistances serious enough to let the horse be unaware of what the rider seeks to obtain.

If the rider is not successful in the first strides, he returns to the walk. Be content, according to the principle, with a single change of lead on one and then the other lead.

When the horse has easily made the changes of lead that way, make the changes while remaining on the track, but still using the rein and leg opposite the requested lead.

If the horse has difficulties changing lead, if his resistances are prolonged, or if he becomes momentarily upset, return to the walk. Re-establish calm and balance and depart again at the canter to try anew the change of lead.

Change of lead by the rein and leg on the side of the requested lead. – As soon as these movements become familiar to the horse, the rider should try to obtain them by the following aids:

To change from left to right, for example, use the right leg and immediately ask for a little half-halt on the right rein.

The right leg must not act at exactly the same time as the hand. The leg pushes forward. The hand receives the weight and gives the position. To accomplish this, the rider must employ little force and put much delicacy into its effects.

At the moment of the change of lead, the horse must not increase his pace. In such a case, stop short; relax (the jaw), then start again.

Decompose (the force and the movement) more than ever for this work. Use minimal or no leg. The horse must change himself. Avoid unbalancing (*renverser*) the horse. Alternate the curb and the bridoon often.

Furthermore, a horse that is well balanced at the canter has almost always enough action such that the rider can use the hand to request a change of lead by acting without the help of the leg. The hand must give the position by a little half-halt applied on the rein on the side of the sought-after lead, which will suffice to produce the change of lead.

Change of lead without the help of the leg. – If the horse has enough action, do not use any leg. This is to avoid the horse being late behind. It is necessary, moreover, to recognize particular cases that may present themselves. Therefore, when, contrary to the above, the horse has little impulsion, and the rider is concerned that after the effect of the hand, there will not remain sufficient impulsion for the change to be made, he must act with the leg first - the leg on the side of the new lead a little more than the other. Then, almost instantaneously, the hand gives the position and movement follows.

But, after a more or less long time, it is still necessary to come to do this work completely without the help of the leg.

When the canter is well regulated, the lightness complete, and the rider judges the action sufficient, he should feel the mouth of the horse carefully so that the effect of the hand has no jerk in it at all, and then act with half-halts (one, two, three, etc., if necessary) on the rein on the side of the requested lead, carrying the hand slightly to the opposite side.

Continue the half-halts, without increasing the force, until the horse has executed the change of lead. In a word, give the *position* which should cause the movement, and do not look for the *movement* which must be a consequence of the position.

If the horse slows, push with the leg, with the spur if needed, until sufficient impulsion is obtained; *but then during the action of the leg, use no action of the hand and do not request the change of lead.* This is an important point.

If the action appears sufficient, give the position. If while giving the position, the action dies, abandon the position, push the horse forward without the hand, with the legs or the spurs, and then give the position again. The movement must come only when the rider has given (the horse) the action and the position.

With a horse from which the half-halts, even only a little marked, take away from the impulsion, limit oneself to a light vibration on the rein on the side of the requested lead while carrying the hand to the opposite side.

Continue the vibration until obtaining the change of lead. But do not use leg during this vibration. The leg would increase the muscle contraction that the hand has met, and then it would be only by a succession of forceful effects, jerky, jarring movements, that the lead changes could be obtained.

In this work, completely release the reins *immediately* when the horse has changed his lead. This is the best way to take count of the effect produced by the hand and to know if equilibrium persists, that is, if too much weight is transferred forward, etc.

Take back the bridoon or the curb with great delicacy when there is need (to rebalance), or to request new changes of lead.

The horse very much appreciates the difference between the complete abandonment of the reins on the neck and the simple descent of the hand during which, even if the reins have no more effect on the mouth, they are nonetheless held at their extremity.

As the training is perfected, the lead changes requested without the help of the leg must be accomplished by simple indications of the reins without any need to have recourse to half-halts or even vibrations.

Lead changes requested by the leg only. – Move on then, as an exercise, to changes of lead requested by the leg without the aid of the hand.

To ask for a change, first hold the reins semi-taut in order to curb as needed any acceleration of the pace.

Then take the reins by their extremity but do not use them unless it is absolutely necessary, and even then their action should be nearly null. Finally, leave the reins entirely on the neck.

One can only say that it is absolutely the leg that has the predominant effect in this work. It is up to the rider's feel; but outside of special cases, it is the leg that is opposite the requested lead that is predominant.

When the legs make the request and the horse's action is augmented, the legs must immediately release. The hand re-establishes the previous cadence, and the legs begin again to give the position. Mix into this work lead changes requested by the hand. Act with extreme delicacy as soon as there is no longer too much weight on the forehand.

A vibration would suffice then, because half-halts would render the horse anxious and hesitant at a time when there is no more need to lighten the forehand.

Requesting lead changes on the leg only serves to restore the forward movement after any work where the hand has been predominant.

Repeated changes of lead. – It is essential that the horse know how to execute *a perfect change of lead,* from left to right and from right to left, at appropriate intervals according to the principles described above.

When the horse can perform these movements in an *irreproachable* manner, there is not much more to his repeating them at short distances, which the rider can then bring closer and closer together so as later to perform changes of lead *au temps* (*a tempi*), a change at each stride of the canter.

To prepare the horse for these exercises that require a great deal of tact and finesse on the part of the rider, he must keep the following recommendations firmly in his mind:

When requesting the lead change, as soon as one feels the action to be sufficient, *begin by bringing the hand closer to the body* (by rotating the wrist, little finger toward the body) so as to shift the weight slightly to the hindquarters, and, only then, carry the hand a little to the side opposite the sought-after lead. Do not press; give the position and *let the horse do it.*

Hold the reins in a single hand (curb or bridoon). Do not carry it too far to the side; nearly no lateral displacement, especially in the repeated lead changes.

The hand marks the half time of a halt in approaching the body (rotating the wrist, little finger toward the body), and it *barely* moves to the right or to the left. But in the beginning, do not fear *to lift the forehand* noticeably with a half-halt that is a little energetic in order to free the shoulders, which are often too loaded for this work.

Carefully feel that the horse is *ready* before asking for the lead changes, push on or slow down as needed, but do not make the hand and legs act at the same time.

If it becomes necessary to decompose (the force and the movement), be *moderate* in the application of half-halts. No jerks, nor even brusqueness. Be very calm. Once the balance is re-established, depart again at the canter and wait a little before asking for the lead change again.

To get to the change of lead every two strides or every stride, ask for only two changes at the start, then come back to the walk. Begin again, and so on. Of course, use only the hand, and try to seize "the moment" ; and lower the hand after each request. Little by little, increase the number of lead changes up to every second stride or every stride. Be careful that the action be sufficient. Be very demanding. Make sure that the fore and hind change exactly at the same time. Use much delicacy in the hand.

If the pace increases, or if the horse panics a little, or if the balance is altered, stop demanding the movement, and as needed, decompose (the force and the movement): halt, and relax (the jaw) before starting again.

When there has been disorder, the training must be already advanced if the rider is to be able to re-establish balance at the canter, or even at the walk.

Above all, avoid demanding this precise work from a horse that is fatigued, annoyed, or overly nervous, or wet with sweat, which would require the work to be accomplished by force. The horse must remain fresh for these difficult lessons, and for him, it must be a game intermixed with rest and reward.

Lead changes on the aids opposite the lead requested, the horse remaining straight in the shoulders and the

haunches. – When a horse departs easily at the canter, *without traversing himself* (going crooked), by means of the rein and leg opposite to the lead required, the rider can also come to obtain the lead change by this same lateral effect while keeping the shoulders and haunches of the horse straight. At the beginning, the rider practices the lead change by these two aids, slightly traversing the horse if necessary.

Then he asks for the lead change, from right to left, for example, in absolutely the same way as has been prescribed to act to make a horse depart from the walk to the canter to the left, without traversing him, by the use of the right rein and leg. The rider must then maintain the horse very straight in the shoulders and the haunches.

Equally, as described above, the rider should endeavor to use the help of the leg as little as possible and to come even to do without it completely. The hand must redouble its finesse, and only scarcely place itself laterally, when it marks its half-time of a halt finished by a kind of pulsation on (the bit on) the side of the requested (new) lead.

***Foule* at the canter.** – To execute the *foule* at the canter, the rider makes canter departs in all directions and on each lead in the middle of the school. He turns often, and very tight. He changes lead, he halts, he departs again, etc. Watch carefully that the position given by the hand does not take away from the impulsion. In such a case, chase the horse forward with the leg before giving the position again.

CHAPTER IV THE *GALOP ALLONGÉ* (EXTENDED CANTER)

Increase the tempo of the canter. – If lightness and the ramener are constant at a moderate canter, the rider should progressively lengthen the gait, taking on successively greater and greater tempo, but at each increase, the pace must be *uniform*, and well regulated, without the horse displacing his head or becoming heavy in the hand. The mobility of the jaw necessarily diminishes as the stride lengthens and the tempo increases. The mobility of the jaw must reappear when the hand acts on the mouth to shift weight to the hindquarters and to induce slowing down.

Exercise the horse in halting from a *galop rapide* (rapid canter or gallop). – The rider will then exercise the horse in halting on the spot from a *grand galop* (large canter or gallop). Recall that for this exercise, before any new demand, the rider must restore lightness, and when he has obtained it and wishes to request a new movement, he must employ an energetic *progressive* force, skillfully graduated, until the achievement of the sought-after result.

It is necessary, therefore, that when the rider asks a horse to halt from the extended canter or the gallop, he must act, very strongly if needed, right away with the hands until the effect of their elevation has produced immobility. Then, he must rein-back *immediately*. By repeating these exercises with thoughtful progression, he will be able to pass easily from the charge to the halt by the simple effect of the hand without using the spur or even the leg.

CHAPTER V JUMPING OBSTACLES

When the rider should begin jumps over obstacles. – He should not jump the horse mounted before his training has given the rider the means to be *absolutely certain* to be able to bring the horse to any object whatsoever, no matter what would be any apprehension that the horse might have.

The *effet d'ensemble* on the spur *alone* allows the rider to force the horse to throw himself at an obstacle that frightens him, or that he does not want to jump. Therefore it is only when the horse has well understood the lesson of the spur that the rider may begin to exercise him at jumps that are higher or wider. Beforehand, the horse must have been accustomed for a long time to jump on the longe or at liberty over all the varieties of obstacles that he could meet under the rider.

After the horse has received this preliminary education and the rider possesses the means certain to prevent the horse from ducking out, and to oblige the horse to

launch himself at no matter what obstacle, there remains only to exercise him methodically to jump mounted over the obstacles that he has been trained to jump without a rider.

One could not recommend too much, for these exercises, to leave the horse free, *for the duration of the jump*, to dispose of his head, his neck, and all his *ressorts* (springs, resources, joints) as his nature inclines him.

CHAPTER VI HABITUATING THE HORSE TO NOISES OF WAR AND TO OTHER FEARSOME OBJECTS

Progression to follow to familiarise the horse with all that frightens him. – To habituate a horse to the noise of drums, of music, and to flags, etc., it is in within the silence of the school, and not outside, that the rider must give the lesson. He must follow an extensive gradation. For the drum for example, the lesson begins with several strikes of the stick. As soon as the horse is disturbed, stop the noise, calm him down, flatter him, start over, etc. Give this lesson with the drummer at the halt at the beginning, and then have the drummer march towards the horse. Everything in progression. For gunfire, hold him far away at the beginning, even very far away, and then approach the shooter almost imperceptibly.

Should the rider happen upon an object that the horse fears, he must guard against trying to approach the object with vigour. On the contrary, let the horse be as far away as he wants from the subject of his fright, and give (the reins) completely. Use the rein and leg as little as possible. Pass and re-pass the object many times, far away to start, and then closer and closer as the horse pays less attention to the object that frightened him in the beginning. To achieve his goal more safely and more quickly, the rider should begin by giving in hand every lesson intended to tame a horse, to reassure him, and to familiarise him with that which worries him or frightens him. See above what is said on this subject in the first part of "Progression of Dressage."

CHAPTER VII FANCY EQUITATION – ARTIFICIAL AIRS

Two ways of acting with the legs. – There are two ways to use the legs when the rider wants to make them act simultaneously and equally.

The first consists of the rider's legs pressing the body of the horse close to their normal position without moving them noticeably. This action of the pushing leg gives impulsion. It also serves to produce the *effet d'ensemble*, which re-establishes balance, when necessary, at every gait, in every position, in all movements, and puts the forces of the horse entirely at the disposal of the rider.

The second way to use the legs is to first put them back a little without touching the horse's coat, and there to apply them softly to the flanks. When the horse has learned to collect himself easily, this effect produces and maintains the engagement of the horse's legs under his body and favours the upward thrust of the hocks, on the condition that the hand require the action (of the horse) to direct itself forcefully upward. Consequently there is an advantage to using this method when the rider requests the piaffe, which is after all only a *rassembler* made regular and cadenced.

But it is only when the piaffe itself becomes easy and very rhythmic that it will suffice to employ the effect in question to produce the piaffe.

How to produce the piaffe. – It is necessary in principle to proceed as follows:

First feel the horse's mouth to assure that the lightness is good and that the horse does not have too much weight on the forehand. Then give (the reins) and request the *rassembler* by little squeezes of the calves repeated successively. Finally, receive in the hand the action produced by the legs, which are released immediately. The hand must not move. It remains *fixed*, and gives (the reins) only when the jaw yields.

Reward by caressing, and halt before the horse stops himself. Use descents of the hand and leg as much as possible. Furthermore, have, as previously, both the bridoon and curb reins knotted so as to be able to alternate their effect at any moment.

When there are resistances or disorder, decompose (the force and the movement). In the beginning, do not seek to re-establish lightness during the piaffe. Halt, and then relax (the jaw). As soon as there is progress, whatsoever lightness there is, reward.

Begin the piaffe on the track on both hands, and then ask for it in the middle of the school. Walk forward after each request. Use very little apparent movement of the leg. If the calves do not have enough effect from their approach, then use an *attaque* (quick press and release, not a bruising or cutting jab) of both spurs without any opposition from the hand to augment the action and wake up the activity. Always avoid the use of this means if the horse twists his tail.

With the action revived, look to cadence it and lengthen the tempo by a soft alternating pressure of the legs. When the cadence has developed, no more hand nor leg.

From time to time, use the whip on the croup to give more elevation to the piaffe, especially if the rider wants to activate the horse's hindquarters. Be very discrete in the use of this means. While one is using it, use no leg, but use descent of the hand. After the use of the whip, which should, when it acts, touch the croup in cadences to mark the tempo, use a little alternating application of the calves.

As this exercise improves, the rider tries to destroy the resistances without halting, but it is still more certain to decompose (the force and the movement) when resistances are prolonged.

Above all in the beginning, it is necessary as much as one can, to avoid making the hand and leg act at the same time so as not *to give rise to* contractions and resistances. In effect, if the action of the hand and that of the leg has been *simultaneous* and equivalent, the horse solicited by two equal and opposite forces, would become immobilised instantaneously.

Let us review the gradation of the rider's demands. Use the hand, to assure lightness. Then leg only. Then, if needed, the hand only, or the leg only. Finally, neither hand nor leg as soon as the horse continues his regular movement himself. Besides that, the rider may leave but only a hardly appreciable interval between the use of the hand and that of the leg.

When, in his piaffe, the horse traverses his croup, it is always because he is opposing a resistance of force to the hand. The traversed croup is *the effect*. *The cause* is a resistance of force. It is necessary to destroy it. The rider does this by a "balancing of weight in the hand, from right to left and from left to right" (Not to be confused with "sawing"), a sort of soft and regular vibration. He begins this balancing during the piaffe, and he continues it as long as required, a long time if it is necessary, even if the horse steps back a little bit. The rider then limits himself to a diminishing intensity of the effect of the hand.

As soon as lightness comes, everything becomes straight; the backward steps cease; the piaffe becomes good.

As we have said, the horse appreciates very well the difference between the descent of the hand with the reins held at their extremity and the complete abandonment of the reins on the neck. But it is above all in the piaffe that the rider perceives it when, after having relaxed the reins totally without the horse advancing, he lets them fall on the neck, which he must do as soon as he can. It happens then often, in the beginning, that the weight shifts to the forehand, which tends to pull the mass in that direction, and the rider is obliged to take back the reins.

The piaffe advancing, or passage. – When the horse piaffes *very well* in place with elevation and cadence, the rider requests the piaffe advancing; this is the *passage*.

In this artificial air the rider should advance only a little: about two or three inches at each stride. For the passage to become regular it must be very soft, the movements must be very rounded, the legs graciously deployed in cadence. It must be the consequence of a concentration of forces of the *rassembler*, and not seem hard for the rider. It has nothing to do with that jerky, stamping, convulsive trot, strongly disagreeable to the rider, to which some often give the same name.

Trot to the rear. – The rider may then move to the piaffe backwards or *trot to the rear*. The same as in the passage, when he must not advance more than about two or three inches at a time, in the trot to the rear each diagonal pair must pose itself only a few centimeters to the rear of the other after having remained a noticeable time in suspension (Faverot, as did many of his contemporaries, believed that there was a slight moment of suspension in the piaffe, a belief not completely discredited until the advent of slow-motion cameras). Change the reins (from bridoon to curb and back) often during this exercise.

Passage on two tracks. – Finally, the rider may begin work on two tracks at the passage; but it is definitely necessary before asking for it that the piaffe be perfect and in place, and that all the movements on the diagonal are being executed admirably at the walk and the collected trot.

One could not recommend too much the greatest tact and discretion in these demands for all this delicate and difficult work. Reward often, and put the most careful gradation into these efforts.

CHAPTER VIII FANCY EQUITATION
– ARTIFICIAL AIRS (*Continued*)

During the preparatory work, when still working in hand, the rider should have made an aide in the saddle request the horse to lift the forelegs alternately, and, finally ask for a little *Spanish walk*. It goes more quickly this way because, if the horse does not understand what was asked of him, the whip of the rider working in hand intervenes to stimulate his obedience. But even when this first lesson has not been given, the mounted rider can still by himself request the lifting of the legs, the *Spanish walk*, and, eventually, the *Spanish trot* by the following means, on condition always that the horse has still been suitably worked during the work in hand.

Extension of the forelegs. – At the halt, make sure that the jaw is softly mobile, then lighten the right shoulder, for example, by slightly elevating and carrying the right hand toward the left in a fashion to operate on the right rein with a half-tension in the direction of the left haunch. Close both legs almost immediately, and when their pressure makes "the forces push forward," oppose the same effect of the hand to the horse's forward movement.

If this ensemble of actions does not cause the lifting and extension of the right foreleg, make the horse understand by touching him on the right shoulder with the whip, or if necessary, on the right forearm. Repeat these elevations of each foreleg until the horse executes them perfectly, and do without the whip as soon as possible.

The Spanish walk. – Then begin the *Spanish walk* by putting the horse at the walk while one of his forelegs is in suspension and well extended. As soon as this leg lands on the ground, inverse the aids to obtain the

elevation and extension of the other. The rider may help himself, if necessary, with the whip. Continue until the gait is frank, easy, with complete extension, and very high with each leg, with the horse remaining very light, of course.

Be careful, above all, that the horse *does not come back on himself* when he lifts a foreleg, whether in place or in movement. He must extend the leg without any backing up, as if he wanted to touch an object placed away from him *in front of* and at the height of his shoulders.

Spanish trot. – The rider can now ask for the *Spanish trot*. The rider must push; strongly activating the horse by an equal and simultaneous pressure of both legs *closed forward* (close to the girth) while the horse is at the Spanish walk with his jaw very flexible.

The rider quickens the walk so as to bring the beats of each diagonal pair of legs closer and closer together, the hand slightly elevated and carried alternately, right and left, to the side opposite from which he looks for extension.

Make generous use of the whip at the beginning. As soon as one has obtained two or three strides of the Spanish trot, come back to the walk, re-establish lightness, and then take the Spanish walk again before asking for the Spanish trot.

When the horse has understood and takes up this artificial air easily, it will no longer be necessary to move the hand laterally. With the legs having acted to produce the Spanish trot with the aid of the whip, receive this impulsion in the hand while elevating it a little. As soon as lightness is manifested, change the reins (from bridoon to curb and back, both having been knotted).

Try to obtain a continuous cadence with a little extension for a step or two while lowering the hand. Halt right away to reward the horse. Demand very little at the beginning. Be content with little. Begin again and try to do away with the hand. Take back the horse as soon as he abandons his balance.

If the speed increases at the moment when the hand lowers, re-establish the balance before anything else; half-halt as needed to prevent the weight from shifting forward. At first, do not abandon the reins entirely. Lower the hand only to raise it again when the pace dies.

In the same way, try to do without the whip for several strides. In other words, look to have the horse support himself and to continue his Spanish trot without aids. A great deal of impulsion is required for this gait. When the rider's legs act, they should not alternate their effect.

With a horse that takes up the Spanish trot easily, it will suffice, in order to produce it, to increase the degree of the horse's action by use of the legs, and that done, to raise the hand to lighten the forehand, marking by soft half-halts the cadence of the first few strides. Then give (the reins), and take back only to maintain the gait if there is need.

The rider can occasionally give clicks of the tongue, but he should do away with any aids, leg, hand, whip, or clicks of the tongue as soon as possible, when the Spanish trot is very energetic, very regular, equilibrium persists; that is, when lightness remains unaltered.

Trot with sustained extension. – To obtain the *trot with sustained extension*, depart at the Spanish trot; ask for the gait while proceeding at a trot that is accelerated but not too quickly. Proceed as always when one wants to have cadence with elevation: first, use the legs to increase impulsion and receive this impulsion in the hand. Use these aids very close together, but as much as possible not simultaneously.

PART FOUR: CONFIRMING THE HORSE

CHAPTER I RAMENER OUTRÉ

The *ramener "outré"* (exaggerated) is nothing other than a *means* to fix the head at the normal ramener by a momentary exaggeration of the demand of the rider. It is only necessary to use it if the rider wants to push the training up to the complete annihilation of the resistances that could present in the mouth and neck, in no matter what position and at whatever would be the gait.

With lightness well established and the head very elevated, move to the ramener outré. – This work should never be undertaken unless the rider can easily obtain the maximum and sustained elevation of the neck at the walk, trot, and canter, with lightness, the jaw yielding at the beginning without movement of the head.

The ramener outré is requested by the bridoon reins and takes place on the track; but the rider must repeat later on the curb the whole progression that we are going to detail here.

The rider begins at the halt. He crosses the bridoon reins in his left hand, the little finger remaining to the outside. The right hand is placed on the right rein. Then the left hand closes "convulsively" while feeling the mouth, but *without pulling*. As soon as lightness is manifested, the hand *follows* the movement of the lowering of the end of the nose.

It continues *to follow* the mouth this way down to the ramener outré; that is, until the moment when the chin comes nearly to touch the chest. If the head, instead of yielding, wants to escape, the hand opposes by contracting with a strong force, but always without pulling on the reins.

In the meanwhile the legs close, the rider comes with the spurs to which, of course, the horse must have been previously been habituated so as to tolerate them without any fuss. He leaves the spurs applied until the complete relaxation of the jaw appears. When this relaxation is produced, the hand experiences the sensation of the complete disappearance of all resistance. At the same time, the tongue lifts the bit, makes it "jump," and sends it against the molars; when the horse is in a simple snaffle, one may hear a characteristic noise, a sort of "crack."

When the hand gives (the reins), the horse's head must remain immobile for a moment, before lifting softly. When the ramener outré has been obtained directly on the bridoon reins, the rider requests it on each of them separately, in a manner to produce an eighth of a lateral flexion of the neck.

The rider can also accelerate the relaxation of the jaw by aiding with the application of the spurs, and by the *support* of the other rein.

Then the rider puts his horse into the ramener outré directly by both reins, and then puts the horse into the walk while fixing his hand to prevent any displacement of the head. The legs do the rest, aided, if needed, by the application of the spurs.

When the ramener outré is well maintained at the walk and easily taken back after the descent of the hand, put the horse into the collected trot while still maintaining the ramener outré. As soon as the relaxation of the jaw is complete, give (the reins) and reward. Apply the spur if it is necessary.

Then, execute canter departs with the ramener outré, and work to achieve relaxation of the jaw at this gait, the same as at the trot. Depart perfectly straight without there being any deviation from the elevation of the head, which must be maintained in ramener outré during the predominating action of one or the other rein, according to the case.

It is quite necessary to notice and remember the sensation felt by the rider when his horse is straight, which must be, on his part, the object of constant care.

For example, if the head and the croup are to the left, with too much weight on the right shoulder, the right rein must, by a tension towards the left haunch, shift the weight to the left. At the same time, *if it is necessary*, the support of the left rein helps the leg on the same side make the croup come back to the right *a little*. But the rider must employ this effect of the leg only in cases in which it does not respond to the rein correction.

Eventually, while at the walk, then at the trot, and then the canter, change from the ramener outré to the maximum elevation of the neck, the head remaining at complete ramener. To do this, elevate the hand without using any force. So as to avoid the discomfort that this movement of the hand causes him, the horse will elevate his neck and become light. Apply the spurs if the relaxation of the jaw does not come or does not persist.

At the various gaits, ask for the eighth of a flexion of the neck while at the ramener outré.

Finally, pass from the halt to the rein-back and from the rein-back to the various gaits, the ramener outré remaining unchanged. Repeat these exercises often.

After that, begin the movements on two tracks in the ramener outré. To change from the lateral movements to the right to the lateral movements to the left for example, carry the hands to the left, make the horse feel the left leg, and when the haunches are well to the right, activate the right leg to depart in the other direction.

Then, request the piaffe in ramener outré. Use no movement of the legs. Use the spur if the horse does not obey the calves. In all the preceding work, the rider must do without the spurs as quickly as possible, then without the legs, and at that moment, play with the reins.

When the relaxation of the jaw is quite complete, the rider will recognize it, as he did when working in hand. The horse will not move his head at all by himself, at the moment of the descent of the hand and will leave it in ramener outré for a certain time.

It is the time now to apply, such as the rider can, the principle of "hand without leg, leg without hand." Afterwards, the rider repeats, as we have described them, all the exercises at the ramener outré on the curb. The elevation of the neck combined with the ramener outré gives and fixes the correct position of the head, which from then on, it never loses, not in the extended gaits, nor in difficult movements.

CHAPTER II THE LITTLE *ATTAQUES*

Confirming the horse in his perfect obedience to the aids. – When the training of the horse has reached its end, it remains only to render him finely tuned (*très fin*) to the aids, so as to have no more need to move, in any apparent fashion, the hand or the leg for the rider to transmit his will to the horse.

The rider's hand must thereafter guard against any action that resembles punishment, such as the half-halt or even the vibration. The rider must act only by indications that are soft, with the wrist fixed. The rider must not take recourse in any rigorous means except to vanquish a resistance that lasts too long.

The rider's legs should be limited to contact with the hair of the coat in their normal place when there is reason to use them. But, *to improve obedience to the calves*, to reawaken the horse's sensitivity, the rider should proceed as follows:

Little *attaques* of the spur. – With the horse confirmed in the knowledge of the spur *and tolerating the spur without any twisting of the tail*, when the rider needs to use the leg, approach the horse delicately with the leg or the calf up to a moderate force, and if that contact does not bring immediate obedience, quickly touch him with the spur or spurs, according to the case. This little *attaque* must be mild, but lively and sudden.

Use the same method if the pace slows, or if a position given by the legs is lost. The legs should fall naturally, and from there not touch the horse unless it is necessary, *as rarely as possible*.

The rider should also avoid the click of the tongue, the whip, or anything that could replace the legs when these things are not absolutely required. After having requested a movement by the hand only, since these actions always retard the forces, it is necessary to dissipate any tendency to *acculement* (come "behind the bit," lose impulsion, or back up) by employing little *attaques* of both spurs at once.

Finally in the piaffe, with the reins semi-taut, after there is mobilization and engagement of the horse's legs, activate him from time to time by use of the spur to obtain higher and more sustained elevation in the cadence. If the horse holds himself back, or if he is not perfectly light, or there is a bit of acculement, *attaque* with both spurs simultaneously to re-establish balance and "to make the forces go forward."

The principle, "leg without hand, hand without leg," must be applied as much as one can, above all in the beginning; but it is not absolute. It is not necessary to erect it into a *system* outside of which there would be assured failure. The rider should limit himself to put it into practice in as much as there is no reason to avoid it, but there comes a moment in the training, and later in the management of the trained horse, when it is, on the contrary, appropriate to unify the effect of the lower aids to that of the upper aids.

So when a horse already very advanced in preparation will not become light on a delicate solicitation of the hand, apply light pressure with the legs, and, if the jaw does not mobilize immediately, quickly come with a little *attaque* of the spurs. Similarly, when the rider wants to demand a halt from one of the various gaits by a simple effect of the hand, the horse must *first* be light. If the jaw resists the opposition of the bit, close the legs delicately, and if lightness does not come instantaneously, use a

little *attaque* of the spurs before demanding the halt.

Thus the rider renders his horse truly *fin aux aides* ("on the aids"), and becomes able to manage him without any apparent movement of the hand or the leg.

It is necessary to be very moderate in the little *attaques* of the spur, to use them only with a great deal of *delicatesse et d'à-propos* (delicacy, timing, and proportion), and to abandon them without hesitation if they provoke a twisting of the tail.

CONCLUSION

The author wanted to reveal in this study *all* of the procedures of dressage used by Baucher at the end of his life.

The author has supposed a horse absolutely stubborn or rebellious, dangerous even, in the work in hand, and he has presented the means to push the horse's education all the way to a sort of *ideal* perfection, which to his knowledge only the horses of Baucher and those of General L'Hotte have attained.

The author has therefore sought to present to the reader an ensemble of measures in which the rider could find the solution to diverse problems of dressage.

It would be an error to believe that a rider really would have to work through every exercise detailed in the *Progression*, and to practice them all with the same care, especially if he has to work a naturally docile and calm horse.

The outdoor rider, the hunter, for example, will do work in hand only as it is indispensable for obedience to the actions of the hand and the indications of the whip. Once in the saddle, he will above all carefully use the same effects of elevation of the neck and head in order to be able, outside, among other horses and despite excitement, to easily shift the horse's weight to the hindquarters by lifting the hand when the horse comes too much on the forehand.

When the horse has lightness, the rider will come to the ramener and consider the training as sufficient when he has completely "taken possession of the head" (*quand il se sera bien "emparé de la tête"*).

If the rider is working an army horse, it is not absolutely necessary to exercise the horse at the *rassembler*, but it is important that the horse be rendered very manageable. It will be necessary therefore, after some exercises in hand for the purpose of facilitating the mobilization of the horse's body in every direction, to work, once in the saddle, at the elevation of the neck that gives balance, and more yet at the turns executed by the pressure of the counter reins (the rein of pressure or neck rein, and the counter rein of opposition in front of the withers or a less extreme form of the neck rein: the second and fourth rein effects. (Licart.))

He repeats these exercises very often at all gaits to obtain great facility in the movement of the forehand around the haunches. These turns by the pressure of the reins are especially useful to the military rider who conducts his horse *with only one hand.*

If the horse is destined for races over obstacles, steeplechase, or stadium jumping, he will have to be rendered very familiar with the effet d'ensemble on the spur, for the rider to have the power *always* to prevent a run-out, and to be sure to master him in all circumstances. Do not forget that in a race the first condition is *fixity* in the suitable position of the head. Any horse that bores on the hand, that *pulls* in an exaggerated fashion *exhausts himself* in useless effort, and so loses some of his chances of winning. Therefore, the rider must render easy the achievement of a relative lightness as a means of shifting weight from the forehand to the hindquarters, and then *s'emparer. . . de la tête* [take hold, with the reins, of the head in its fixed position] at fast gaits.

On the contrary, if the rider wants to do school equitation with as much development as possible of *loftiness*, he must take great care with the "concentration of forces," the *rassembler*.

After having obtained lightness by relieving the

forehand, he moves to the ramener outré, which permits him to stabilize the head in an unvarying position, despite the quest for artificial airs and the most difficult of movements.

Remember that for any horse specifically destined to the outdoors, it is most particularly the elevation of the head and neck that must be sought after and obtained so as to eventually come to conserve the ramener, even at the extended gaits, and that once this result is obtained, the training is sufficient.

In contrast, if the rider is aiming for higher (*savante*: learned) equitation, he must follow the path more scrupulously and task himself with all that can facilitate the *rassembler*, which alone gives loft to the movements and brilliance to their execution.

The wiser the horse and the more modest the rider in his demands, the more likely the rider can simplify the training and reduce the number of means used.

DRESSAGE OF THE OUTDOOR HORSE

Advice Given to Members of "L'Étrier[1]"
by General Baron FAVEROT DE KERBRECH
Recalled by one of his students:
By General George de Lagarenne.

---

[1] "THE STIRRUP" Riding Club

Foreword

General Baron Faverot de Kerbrech, one of the premier horse trainers of his age, was also an incomparable riding master. While remaining faithful to the methods of Baucher, whose teaching he had received directly, he knew enough to extract the essential principles from this somewhat dense doctrine, and his personal experience brought him a concept of equitation at once wise and practical, a concept in which the principal characteristic is the simplicity of the means.

In 1891, The General (Faverot) published *Methodical Dressage of the Saddle Horse, From the Last Teachings of F. Baucher, Recalled by One of his Students*. This very interesting work, which, originally, Faverot did not want to sign, in order to be self-effacing before his illustrious master, was above all an homage rendered to Baucher. Faverot wanted "to prevent the lessons of this learned master, (Baucher) from being misunderstood, unknown, or most of the time made a travesty of, threatened with disappearance without leaving a trace."

Nevertheless, *Methodical Dressage of the Saddle Horse* bears the personal imprint of Faverot, as much by its order and clarity as by certain new ideas that are expressed therein.

These principles, which The General (Faverot) has consecrated in this book, were made known to those around him, and he excelled at explaining them and commenting on them. How many officers, students, and friends retain imperishable memories of his precious lessons? Recognition is due him by the members of the equestrian society, *l'Étrier* (the Stirrup), who during the last years of his life, had the privilege of receiving his teaching. Those Monday morning meetings at Pellier's or in the Tattersall school remain unforgettable.

Active duty officers, retired officers, former trainers from Saumur, sportsmen, huntsmen, fans of higher-level dressage, laureates of stadium jumping, habitués of the Allée des Poteaux, to which were joined sometimes a graceful *amazone* (gifted or trained female rider), riders of very different ages and tastes, but all united by their common passion for the horse, were among the general's ordinary audience. Such was the parade (*reprise*) he liked to direct, a parade that sometimes had the honor to be led by that other remarkable trainer, also taken by a premature death, General Bellegrade.

Nothing could reproduce the charm of those moments when, enveloped in a lively conversation and studded with anecdotes, the advice took shape and was repeated in its most attractive form. With what pleasure we would hear the master correcting errors with a courteous indulgence, showing the most rebellious riders the way, and encouraging the sometimes painful efforts of beginners just as much as the results quickly attained by the veterans.

Regarding high school, high level equitation, there was hardly a question about his retrospective point of view. What the general wanted was above all to put in a form suitable to take home all of the simple methods by which an ordinary rider could render a horse agreeable to ride.

Just as one would hit a nail for a long time to sink it deeply, he would insist relentlessly on essential principles, each time expressed and developed under a new form after their application. Little by little these principles were engraved into the students' minds and there would take on the solidity of the Gospel.

Yielding to the solicitations of the audience of l'Étrier, the general wrote for them a few pages which summarized this practical knowledge, and signed them, giving them a title that stated the goal pursued in those lessons:

There exists no guide more precious for the rider desirous of "making" a horse that has already been started without having aspirations for the delicacies of higher-level equitation. Is it not here that most of us find ourselves? We buy at a public sale, we choose at a sales yard, we take into the ranks a horse of whatever sort, and we try to make a hack, a hunter, or a charger that is agreeable and manageable in any circumstance.

How rare are those who start the thankless task to make a colt that "hasn't carried anything but flies" ? How many are they, who by inclination push training beyond normal limits, who consent to enclose themselves regularly between the walls of the school so that the young people of the current generation can "grind away" (*gratter*) in an inelegant fashion and with a touch of disdain? One may easily understand why the general would limit himself in his counsel, holding himself voluntarily equidistant between the two poles of equitation, breaking-in and high school.

These notes that in their form at the time were not intended for publication he saved to complete them later and to edit them. They have the merit of sober concision and, devoid of any discussion, of any embellishment; the method appears very clear and quite luminous.

Consequently, it is with the certainty of being useful to my comrades in the cavalry, and to all fervent equestrians, that I have asked the son of our venerated master for the authorization to edit this little book. It is also with the desire to settle, in the name of l'Étrier (The Stirrup Club), a debt of recognition and with the thought that this posthumous publication will be a new homage to the memory of General Faverot de Kerbrech.

-General George de Lagarenne

DRESSAGE OF THE OUTDOOR HORSE

INTRODUCTION

Many good riders who love above all the outdoors cannot or will not practice the advanced and methodical procedures indispensable to making a school horse or to training a fundamentally stubborn horse. They would be enchanted to simply provide basic training for a horse that is already broken in and no longer presents any serious difficulties.

It is for them that we have written the few lines that follow.

To make (*mettré*, to put) a horse is to place his head; it is to render him light to the hand, obedient to the leg, easy to turn, and very regular in his gaits. One arrives at this by the application of a very few means, often repeated. The most important means are: the "lateral effects," the "turn on the neck rein," and the "rein-back." The rider pursues "lightness" as a consequence of these means.

Lightness must be the constant preoccupation of the rider. – The quest for and the preservation of lightness must be the constant preoccupation of the rider because it alone indicates that his mount is in balance.

A horse is light to the hand when – in-hand or mounted, at the halt or in motion – a half-tension on one of the reins of either the bridoon or the curb, or on both reins employed simultaneously, provokes the soft mobility of the jaw without the mouth opening in a noticeable fashion. The horse's tongue makes the two bits jump, one against the other, making an argentine sound.

These conditions together constitute a type of ideal lightness. Even if these conditions are always to be sought by the rider, ideal lightness can only be obtained in entirety at the halt or at slower gaits (*petites allures*, small gaits). In the measure that the tempo increases, the mobility of the jaw greatly diminishes only to disappear completely in a race or at the (cavalry) charge.

Ideal lightness is attained while at the speed of a rapid gallop when the mouth does not weigh on the hand in a bothersome way. Above all, the head should remain steady. We will explain this later.

"Lateral effects." – The "lateral effects," use of the rein and leg on the same side, are those that the rider uses instinctively when he has to defeat an unexpected resistance. The action of the rein of either the bridoon or the curb relaxes the jaw, and the continuation of this action produces the ramener; the leg on the same side contributes by obtaining lightness by displacing the croup as needed and by removing the point of support for the resistances. The leg is helped in return by the opposition of the direct rein to the divergence of the haunches. The lateral effects have the great benefit of engagement of the hind leg on the same side, the lowering of the haunches, favouring the degree of collection that is necessary at the various gaits. The lateral effects provide a means to prevent most defences by the facility that they give to stabilize the horse's head, and to prevent the hind leg from sticking to the ground.

"Turns on the neck rein." – The rider must become a master of the turn on the "pressure of the rein" which at his will shifts the weight of the neck toward one of the shoulders and displaces the forehand in that direction. The confirmation of the ramener is essential in riding with one hand.

"Rein-back." – Finally, by the "rein-back" the rider makes the shifting of weight onto the hindquarters easy and improves lightness in the hand.

PROGRESSION

1. Work in hand

Request lightness with the bridoon; then with the curb; then with each isolated rein of the curb and the bridoon. – In hand, the rider teaches the horse lightness first on both bridoon reins, then on both curb reins, then on each isolated rein of the bridoon and the curb.

The rider places himself facing the horse. Put the thumb of each hand into a ring of the bridoon, and lift the head and neck by acting on the corners of the lips, but avoid making the horse back up. As soon as the jaw relaxes, give.

Then take a shank of the curb or a curb rein in each hand, and seek the same mobility of the jaw while lifting the head and neck. Avoid making the horse back up so that the rider is only requesting lightness.

Give (the reins), as soon as lightness is obtained.

Next take, one at a time, each rein of the curb and then each rein of the the bridoon and hold near the bit and request the relaxation of the jaw, on the right and then on the left by an effect of elevation, and lightly bring the end of the nose to the side on which the rider is working.

If the rider encounters a somewhat prolonged *"mutism"* of the jaw, he stands on one side of the horse, takes a bridoon rein in one hand and the curb rein in the other, on the same side. He carries the bridoon hand forward while the other hand softly activates the curb in such a fashion as to delicately invite the horse to unclench his teeth and make his bits jump with his tongue.

As soon as the relaxation of the jaw is produced, of course, give (the reins).

Teach the horse to respond with lightness to the half-tension of an isolated rein of the curb, or of the bridoon, or two by two. Do not seek the ramener yet. It will come later, quite naturally, from the saddle.

Make the croup yield to the right and to the left from the whip. – Make the croup yield to the right and to the left from the whip so that the haunches pivot around the shoulders. Be content with a very slight displacement of the croup.

Repeat these steps of "reverse pirouettes" often.

Rein-back. – Request the rein-back *by elevation* of the head on the bridoon or the curb.

Transfer the weight from forehand to hindquarters by repeating often these elevation effects that bring about the rein-back. The less the horse steps back at each request, the better is the work.

Ensure the horse is absolutely straight. If he throws his haunches to one side, counter this mistake by carrying the forehand to the same side. If all goes well, spend only one day on the work in hand. As soon as the rider gets lightness and the reverse pirouettes and rein-back are performed easily with the horse relaxed and calm, send him back to the stable.

2. Lesson in Mounting

If everything went well the day before, begin the lesson by repeating the work in hand, and immediately move to the first lesson in mounting. This lesson must always be given with the greatest care. Done well, it makes the horse make enormous progress.

To start this work, stand at the horse's head. Instruct an aide to approach the stirrup, to put his foot into it, to lift himself and to arrive in the saddle with a careful progression, stopping himself as soon as the horse is disquieted. While this is going on, correct any movement by the horse with little tugs {*saccades]* in order to get his attention and to dominate him.

As soon as the horse manifests calm and confidence, flatter him with gesture and voice. The secret of this lesson consists of stopping any appearance of resistance or revolt, but reward submission as soon as the horse shows it.

When the horse accepts mounting without difficulty, the rider dispenses with the help of the aide and puts himself in the saddle. Correct any tendency toward nervousness or rebellion using, according to the principle, little saccades taken on the reins. Do not walk on until the horse is absolutely calm while being mounted. With certain horses whose spirit is problematic, it is beneficial to walk them in hand, or to longe them for a while before each dressage lesson. Before allowing him to move, execute the following work in place.

3. Working the horse in place

At the halt, from the saddle, request lightness on the various reins. – Request lightness by lifting the hand a little, first on both bridoon reins, then on both curb reins, then each rein isolated (of the bridoon or of the curb). Give (the reins), as soon as there is mobility of the jaw.

The effect of pressure on the neck. – When lightness has been obtained on an isolated rein, by lifting the hand a little, take a half-tension on this same rein toward the diagonally opposite hind leg.

Thus produce, successively on each rein of the curb or of the bridoon, a slight *pli* (bend) by bringing the end of the nose to the side of the semi-taut rein to shift the weight of the neck to the other shoulder.

As soon as lightness is manifested by the soft mobility of the jaw, give (the reins) immediately. Repeat these exercises several times.

This effect of an isolated rein prepares the horse for turns with pressure on the neck and brings the head to the vertical. It leads to the ramener, and must therefore be repeated and practiced with particular care.

Habituate the horse to obey each leg. – Habituate the horse to obey the legs. The rider takes a single rein (the bridoon first, then the curb) in each hand. He lifts both hands and presses lightly with the leg (on the same side as the rein that is contacted) on the flank of the horse.

Method to "oppose the shoulders to the haunches." – If obedience to this aid takes too long, the rider opens the rein on the same side (as the leg that is applied), in a fashion to "oppose the shoulders to the haunches" without upsetting the position of the horse's head. This rein effect to oppose the shoulders to the haunches finds its application throughout training and any time that the horse shows a hesitation to go forward. It is completely different from the one that has as its objective to shift the weight of the neck to the right or to the left. The latter effect is obtained by a half-tension on a rein toward a diagonally opposite hind leg, while the effect of opposition to the haunches is produced by opening the hand toward a line perpendicular to the axis of the horse.

Many riders confuse these effects in practice without realizing it, so they cause resistances that remain inexplicable to them, and more insurmountable, as they unconsciously increase these resistances by adding intensity to an action that, in their mind, should destroy the resistances. For example, when a horse displaces his croup to the right, while turning his nose to the right, any effect of the right rein not made by pushing the hand well to the right, without pulling, will result in the shifting of the weight of the neck to the left shoulder. Pulling on the right rein will cause the escape of the haunches to the right and the exaggerated placing of the head to the right.

Making the jaw yield by the displacement of the croup. – When the rider requests lightness on one rein alone, if the relaxation of the jaw takes too long, the most practical means of achieving the relaxation consists of displacing the croup by the pressure of the leg on the same side, and continuing this methodical rotation of the haunches around the shoulders until lightness is manifested.

The reason this works is that *in the riding horse, all his resistance has its point of support in the croup*. By preventing the hindquarters from sticking to the ground, the rider prevents the possibility of resistance and thus brings on the relaxation of the jaw.

Habituating a nervous horse to the calves without overexcitement. – Certain horses fear the legs. They show an exaggerated sensitivity when the rider applies them to the flanks. With these horses, the rider must stop this nervousness before anything else by making them feel both calves at the halt, and by preventing, by opposition of the hand, any instinctive or disorderly movements. The rider leaves the calves in contact with the flanks as long as inquietude manifests itself by stamping or movement. When calm appears, give completely.

The rider must give this lesson with plenty of tact and take plenty of time. He must not be afraid to put a certain force into the embrace of the legs at the start, and to continue until he has a very strong grip and the horse remains quiet. In this way, the rider will take away any fear of the legs from the horse.

He will prevent the *"faux finesse"* that he must not confuse with the true tuning to the aids, which is manifested by a gentle tranquil obedience, proportioned to the touch of the rider.

In principle, he should leave his legs on the flanks of the horse as long as the horse is impressionable so that the horse finishes by no longer paying attention as long as pressure of the legs does not increase to convey a new demand from the rider.

Make the rein-back methodically. – When the croup yields easily to the action of each leg, let the horse rest in place for a moment. Next request the rein-back by a simple effect of lifting the hands, which at the same time are carried a little to the rear. Thus obtain a backward movement step by step, very slowly, on the bridoon, then on the curb, with no action by the legs. If the croup is carried to one side, oppose this displacement by opening the rein on the same side very frankly (opposition of the shoulders to the haunches). With the rein-back coming easily, very straight, the horse remaining very light, ask for the walk forward as explained below.

4. Work at the Walk

Ask for lightness on the various reins at the walk. – With the horse light (on the bridoon or on the curb), having closed the legs and lowered the hand a little, walk on.

While at the walk, request lightness frequently, without at first requiring the *mise en main* (put in hand, the ramener with relaxation of the jaw, "on the bit") and without using the legs.

To this end, work the various reins successively; on both of the bridoon to begin; then on both of the curb; then separately on each rein (of the bridoon and then the curb) semi-taut. If the lightness is late to appear, halt; give (the reins) slightly, as described above, and depart again.

Exercise the horse on the lateral effects. – When the rider can easily obtain lightness at the walk acting on each rein alone (of the bridoon and of the curb), begin to request, at the same time and without changing direction, a little yielding of the croup on a slight pressure of the leg on the same side as the active rein.

These "lateral effects" should result in bringing the end of the nose to the side of the semi-taut rein and driving the haunches slightly (only a few centimeters) to the opposite side. The whole body of the horse should pivot around the left foreleg if the lateral effect is on the left or around the right foreleg if the effect is on the right.

The rider walks the horse forward several steps in the slightly bent and lateral position that is the result. Then he straightens the horse. Of course the rider should have the opposite rein and leg in contact during the lateral effects. They must be attentive and ready to intervene to correct the effect of an excess of intensity, always possible in the use of the two principal aids.

The repetition of this exercise results in rendering the horse obedient to the legs, bringing the end of the nose closer to the vertical leading to the ramener, and causing a certain engagement of the horse's hind leg on the side of the active leg, bringing the horse to sit (lower his croup), and to produce the beginnings of the "*rassembler.*"

The rider should intersperse the lateral effects, executed this way, with the walk on the straight, and repeat them alternatively on the right rein and leg and on the left rein and leg. The rider should do these exercises once or twice per lesson until they are performed easily and they have become well understood by the horse.

Begin "turns on pressure on the neck." – Then the rider moves to "turns on pressure on the neck."

With the horse walking forward, made light on the half-tension of one of the left reins, for example, toward the right hock, and while lifting the hand without action from the leg, increase the pressure of this rein on the neck with the end of the nose kept to the left.

If the horse obeys this pressure by letting his shoulders "fall" to the right, by smoothly carrying his forehand in this direction, the turn is drawn on the arc of a circle of small radius. If the pressure of the rein produces a slight slowing, make the horse feel the calf on the same side. If the slowing persists, stop all rein pressure; re-establish the gait with the legs. Begin again with the pressure of the semi-taut rein on the same side as before.

As soon as the rider achieves a turn on a very small circle this way, he stops the aid and gives completely. If the sought-after effect is not easily obtained, the rider can help himself a little at the beginning with the rein (bridoon or curb) on the side to which he is turning, but he should avoid using it as soon as it is no longer absolutely necessary.

In the same way, if the application of the left rein, for example, produces an exaggerated bend to the left, he should act at the same time with the right rein, but with enough discretion so that the effect of the pressure of the left does not cease to be determinant.

Afterward, request the turn on a small circle on the other hand, and repeat to the left the work that was done to the right. The lateral effect and the work on small circles produce the ramener quite naturally when the rider executes them using the curb reins.

Ramener on both curb reins. – The moment has come now to seek the "mise en main" on straight lines by making both curb reins act at the same time, and without using the legs.

If the half-tension of these two reins produces the ramener and lightness, give (the reins) immediately. If a slowing is produced, stop the action on the reins and re-establish the gait with the legs.

If lightness is delayed or disappears momentarily, retrieve it with the lateral effects explained above (rein and leg on the same side until the croup yields slightly while moving forward), and by the rein procedure that leads to turns on small circles.

IMPORTANT RECOMMENDATIONS

The rider should fix in his mind the following recommendations, which are universally applicable.

a) Confirm the ramener by the simultaneous use of one curb rein (or bridoon) and one bridoon rein (or curb) on the opposite side. – When the horse responds to the lateral effects, it is beneficial, if the rider requests lightness on one rein of the bridoon, for example, to take a feel at the same time on the opposite curb rein, and reciprocally, at the same time that a curb rein is used as the principal aid, to act with the bridoon rein on the other side. This crisscrossing of the rein effects, executed without the help of the legs, relaxes the jaw and confirms the ramener. They should be from this moment onward practiced from time to time throughout the training.

b) Work with the reins very short. – From this time onward, it is not necessary to fear working with very short reins, showing oneself to be strict, without the use of the legs, and without causing a slowing of the pace when using one or both reins. As soon as lightness comes, the rider must give and leave the horse free. He takes back his reins, of course, if the heads moves out of place, if the neck lowers, if the speed increases, or if the balance is altered. If the effect of the reins slows the pace, stop all action of the hand, and use the legs to correct this fault.

c) Seek perfect straightness in the horse. – The rider cannot forget that one of the preoccupations of dressage must be to have his horse absolutely straight in the shoulders, the haunches, the neck, and the head. To the degree that the procedures indicated above render the horse more supple and more obedient, the bend of the neck produced by the application of the reins should become less and less noticeable, thanks to the eventual co-ordination of the opposite rein.

d) Straighten the horse by the rein on the neck. – Finally, when a horse is bent naturally to one side (the croup and the head to the same side)-something that happens often – one should not straighten him with the legs: that is work without end. There is only one efficient means to put him straight. That is, if he has the end of his nose and his haunches to the right, for example, to make him very familiar with the effect of the left rein on the neck, in a manner to give him, at the will of the rider, a bend to the left and thus to make his shoulder "fall" to the right. In other words, it is in pushing the weight of the neck, and consequently the forehand, to the right that the rider obtains, on a supple horse, the shift of the haunches to the left, and not in looking to push, by using the right leg, the croup to the left without modifying the faulty disposition of the forehand.

The actions of the reins that are in question here demand tact and delicacy. They must be repeated often during the whole course of training, but they yield tangible results to the persevering and conscientious rider.

Correct lightness increases impulsion. – Before moving to the work at the trot, it is important for the rider to establish in his mind, once and for all, that what must happen, from the point of view of impulsion, is the search for and the conservation of lightness.

One day, General von Hammel, then Equerry (Master of Horse) to the King of Wurtemberg, had us ride at Stuttgart several horses from the Royal Stables. He told us, "I want any horse trained by me to *pull his carriage well* (*tire bien sa voiture*) under the rider." He meant by that, a ridden horse must "go frankly into the collar" (*donner franchement dans le collier*) consequently to attack the terrain with all four legs as if he had a carriage to pull behind him, while remaining light in the mouth. The image appears original and right to us. We have held on to it.

So, when lightness is obtained on single reins (one after the other) held short, as we have described, that produces the ramener and the engagement of the hind legs.

It results in a balanced state such that the littlest action of the leg determines, according to the case, the progression or acceleration of the pace. The horse is so much more disposed to carry himself forward, to animate himself, that any fear of the hand disappears, due to the sole fact that he savors his bit, that he is truly light.

Therefore nothing opposes his straight forwardness any more, and he gains as much in impulsion as his lightness is more complete and confirmed. In recommending working with reins a little short, we also intend to avoid the habit of riding with floating reins, with reins "in a garland."

We are not less in favor of descent of the hand practiced when the horse is in perfect balance, but on the condition that neither the head nor the neck are displaced, and that immediately afterward the rider comes back to a normal half-tension on the reins, which will allow him to feel whether lightness persists or has changed or has disappeared.

Then, if the training has been successful, the horse comes – in pulling his carriage – to give in the hand, to seek his lightness himself by mobilizing his jaw, more or less according to his pace, when he encounters the bit.

That is what allows us to say not only that correct lightness does not extinguish impulsion, but that, on the contrary, it puts forwardness into horses that possess it and hold it easily.

During all the work at the walk, halt very often; then immediately rein back methodically, and as soon as the rider has obtained a backward stride very easily with a good mobility of the jaw, depart again at the walk.

5. Work at the Collected Trot (*petit trot*)

Execute at the collected trot all the work done at the walk. – When the work at the walk is well executed, as described above, the rider repeats the exercises at the collected trot. He can even begin the trot before the preceding exercises are completely understood by the horse.

But if the rider wants to make progress quickly, it is preferable not to take up the trot until the horse has perfectly understood, and regularly executed at the walk, all that has been detailed above.

The progression is the same at the trot as at the walk.

The rider begins by requesting lightness on the various reins without seeking the ramener. Then he moves to the "lateral effects" and "turns on the pressure of the rein" which produce the mise en main naturally.

He should also teach the horse from the walk in lateral movements on a lateral effect to take the trot during these movements.

He finishes by the lesson of the ramener, requested on both curb reins acting at the same time and without the help of the legs.

As at the walk, halt often, rein back, and as soon as lightness is complete, depart again to the trot. Before starting the lengthened trot, it is a good thing to take the horse through the line of exercises that make up the work at the canter.

6. Work at the Canter

Request the canter depart while giving the position by the "lateral effect." – With the horse at the walk, bend him slightly to the left and diagonal to the line of travel (left lateral effect); put him into the canter to the right, still making the action of the left rein and leg primary.

The canter thus obtained, re-straighten the horse by the pressure of the left rein on the neck, and make him light by the left lateral effect, before returning to the walk. Do the same work on the right lateral effect to obtain the canter to the left.

Canter depart on a small circle on the pressure of the outside rein, aided by the leg on the same side. – As soon as the departs requested that way become familiar to the horse, put him on a small circle to the right, for example, by means of the pressure of the left rein (*tourner par appui*, turn by pressure or turn by neck rein), and obtain the canter to the right, passing through the trot as needed, but always using the left rein and leg as the principal agents.

The left rein must be the predominant aid, and it must push the mass to the right with the end of the horse's nose remaining to the left.

The rider's left leg, while still communicating the necessary action, must avoid traversing the horse so that his shoulders and haunches, therefore, remain on the circle being described. Once the horse is at the canter, make him light before coming back to the walk.

Finally obtain the depart on the straight, still on the lateral aids opposite the requested lead. – As soon as this work is complete and executed well to the right and to the left, the rider should move to the canter depart on a straight line. With the horse remaining straight in the shoulders and the haunches, request the canter still using as the principal aids, the rein and leg opposite the requested lead.

The idea is first to give the horse the position by shifting weight slightly toward the hindquarters, and then to push him to the right and forward.

To do this, with the horse light and in ramener, to request the canter to the right for example, departing from the walk or the trot, lift the hand and bring it toward the body (by rotation of the wrist) in a sort of "half-halt," the left rein acting nearly alone with a progressive intensity deftly graduated; and end this effect by carrying the hand to the right in a manner to produce on the neck with the same left rein a slight pulsation to the right. But at the moment when the hand begins the effect in question, the left leg acts with a pressure proportionate to the necessary increase in action.

The pressure of the left rein on the neck tends to produce a certain bend to the left, to make the croup move slightly to the left, while the shoulders are pushed to the right. The delicate pressure of the left leg should not traverse the horse at all. In addition, the right rein and leg must always be ready to intervene if necessary.

With the (canter) depart on the straight being successful and very well done, request the turns on the neck rein at the canter. But never come back to the walk without having obtained lightness by using, as needed, the lateral effects or even just the pressure of the outside rein. Just as at the walk and trot, intersperse into the canter work frequent halts followed by a methodical rein-back, and do not depart again until one has thus obtained good lightness. Do not forget that in any lateral effect with the goal of relaxing the jaw, the rein must be employed as it has been explained, to oppose the shoulders to the haunches, that is, most importantly, by moving the hand sideways.

7. Work at the lengthened trot (*grand trot*)

With the various canter departs working well, the rider should go back to the work at the trot, then work the horse at the lengthened trot on straight lines and circles.

If lightness and the ramener change, ask for them again on the lateral effects, a little more energetically than at the collected trot, and by turns on the neck rein.

8. Change of lead at the canter

Request the change of lead by the same means as the canter departs. – If the rider wants to push the education of the horse all the way to the (flying) change of lead, he must ask for it by the same means as the canter departs. Therefore, with the horse at the canter to the right, the rider starts by asking for the lead change by using the lateral effect on the right, traversing the horse slightly as needed.

Next, with the horse having understood what was asked of him, the rider puts him on a circle to the right, for example, and at the moment when he wants to change the circle, he asks for the change by a pulsation of the right rein on the neck, aided slightly by the right leg, but in a fashion to make the forehand sort of "fall" to the left. The change of lead obtained, he comes back to the walk.

When the rider has succeeded several times in this exercise, the moment comes to ask the horse for the lead change on a straight line, without failing to remain straight in the shoulders and the haunches. The rider proceeds to change from the right lead to the left, for example, absolutely the same way as has been explained above to put the horse to the canter to the left on the straight line, and without traversing him.

9. Exercise at the *galop rapide* (gallop)

Working at the gallop without displacement of the head, and with relative lightness. – When the horse remains light and in the ramener at the *galop ordinaire* (canter) and at the lengthened trot, it is time to exercise him at the *galop rapide* (gallop).

The rider progressively lengthens the canter (to the gallop) while fixing the hands low and separating the curb reins (or the bridoon reins), or even taking in one hand a bridoon rein and in the other a curb, or finally, in each hand both a curb rein and a bridoon rein, in a fashion to be able to better master the horse's head, and

to be able to act with lateral effects if the ramener is lost, or should the horse pull.

The rider must come to the point where, by using these effects skillfully, he can push the gallop to full speed without the head moving, without the horse escaping the mise en main, and without the contact becoming exaggerated.

Then the rider slows progressively in a fashion to return to a moderate and cadenced canter without the horse ceasing "to give his head." He re-establishes complete lightness then by the lateral effect, and if necessary by turns on the neck rein.

10· The *Rouler* (to roll)

The means used for the *"rouler"* are the same as those to put the horse at the canter (or gallop) on the lateral aids without traversing him. – When the rider gallops at speed, at the end of a race for example, it is perfectly useful to *"rouler"* a horse to tempt him to make the greatest speed of which he is capable at the moment when he seems at the end of his strength and wind.

Now, the rouler is nothing other in sum than the repeated use, at each stride, of the means indicated above to put the horse at the canter (or gallop) on a straight line without traversing him, making use of the rein and leg on the side opposite the lead requested.

At the end of each stride of the gallop, the rider must relieve the forehand by a rapid effect, first carrying the hands a little back while lifting them slightly, then immediately pushing them toward the lead on which the horse is galloping, and forward so as to push in some way the mass in that direction at the same time as the legs act vigorously at the flanks.

In a race, the rider must strive to feel on which lead the horse is galloping; what is more, it is relatively easy to recognize, at the moment of the depart, if he has embarked on the right or left, and later down the course, if he has changed his lead or has become disunited This observation is important because if the rider "rolls" toward the left, for example, a horse that is galloping to the right, far from accelerating his speed, the rider will prevent him from using all his resources.

CONCLUSION

We have looked for simplicity and unity in these procedures. We wish that from the first to the last day of training the rider use the same aids to request the same movements, the canter depart for example.

One may remark that we have not spoken of work – prolonged – *sur les hanches* (on the haunches, collected usually on two tracks). That is because we judge the "movements" on two tracks useless for what we seek. We think that the progression detailed above is sufficient to teach a horse to respond to the leg. Furthermore, it puts him in a state to execute, if it is desirable after a short preparation, any figure, and any air of the school on two tracks on a straight line or on a circle.

As to the *"pli"* (bend, usually a slight bend), the lateral placement of the head toward the hand on which the horse is moving, the search for which tends to put the horse *de travers* (crooked, askew), and has as a consequence the use of diagonal aids, useful to produce the pli but impractical at rapid gaits, we believe that it is necessary to abandon this pli as an error of the past, inapplicable to the equitation of the outdoors.

In addition, we do not pretend to impose on anyone our way of seeing things. It is in practice that one judges theories. If riders of good will would try these procedures, they will see whether we are right.

GLOSSARY

French: English

acculement: get behind the aids, back up, haunches leading

appuyer: half-pass

arriere-main: hindquarters

attaques des eperons: application of the spurs

avant-main: forehand

descents de main et des jambs: descent of the hand and legs; self-carriage.

décontracté: de-contracted, relaxed

half pirouette: half pirouette

deux pistes: two tracks

dressé: dressed, straightened, trained

effet d'ensemble: coordinated effect, effect of the whole

fait tomber: makes to fall, the forehand towards the centre of the circle.

forcer le mouvement: the rider must *progressively* increase the effect of the bit so that the horse feels it with an intensity growing almost imperceptibly,

les forces s'eloignent trop: the forces have gotten too far away

foule: crowd, work in the school at the same time as a group of other riders, each doing a separate exercise

manège: riding school, arena, usually rectangular

mise en main: put in hand, the ramener with relaxation of the jaw; "on the bit" *pas de coté*: steps to the side; lateral movements

pirouettes ordinaires: ordinary pirouettes, turns on the haunches

pirouettes renversées: reversed pirouettes, turns on the forehand

principe d'acculement: any degree of the haunches leading

ramener: flexion of the head and neck at the poll with the forehead at or approaching the vertical.

ramener outré: ramaener exaggerated; over-flexion with the chin coming toward the chest.

rassembler: the mobilizing of the hindquarters to bring them under the mass of the body without necessarily advancing, sitting the horse.

reculer: rein-back

ressorts: springs, joints, resources

rétivité: inveterate rebelliousness

rouler: to roll, repeated lateral canter aids, outside rein and leg, to encourage the gallop.

saccade: a tug on the reins or the longe line on the cavesson usually upwards to raise the head or to discipline the horse, proportional to the resistance.

galop sur les hanches: very collected canter, usually on two tracks.

tient les hanches: holds the haunches, half-pass

trot enlevé: rising trot

BIBLIOGRAPHY

Licart, *Assiette et Emploi des Aides*,

Fédération Française de Sports Équestres, undated, pages 13-16

F. Baucher, *New Method of Horsemanship*, 9th edition, in Hilda Nelson, *François Baucher, The Man and his Method*, J. A. Allen & Co. Ltd, London 1992

Dominic Ollivier, *Equitation: Flexions et Dressage à Pied*, Chiron, Paris 1997

www.ingramcontent.com/pod-product-compliance
Lightning Source LLC
Chambersburg PA
CBHW050553300426
44112CB00013B/1897